Institute of Classical Architecture & Art
20 West 44th Street, Suite 310, New York, NY 10036
Telephone: (212) 730-9646 Facsimile: (212) 730-9649
www.classicist.org

Russell Windham, Chairman
Peter Lyden, President
Classicist Committee of the ICAA Board of Directors:
Anne Kriken Mann and Gary Brewer, Co-Chairs;
Michael Mesko, David Rau, David Rinehart, Suzanne Santry

Guest Editor: Marc Appleton

Managing Editor: Stephanie Salomon
Design: Suzanne Ketchoyian

DEDICATION

This issue of the *Classicist* is dedicated to three historians whose writings have illuminated Southern California's cultural and architectural heritage for so many of us: Kevin Starr, 1940–2017, California State Librarian; David Gebhard, 1927–1996, Professor of Architectural History, University of California, Santa Barbara; and Robert Winter, Professor Emeritus, Occidental College.

ACKNOWLEDGMENTS

The ICAA, the *Classicist* Committee, and the Guest Editor wish to thank the essay writers and the anonymous peer reviewers for their contributions to *Classicist* No. 15. We extend our gratitude to David Wakely and Architectural Resources Group for our front cover photograph, Matt Walla for the back cover photograph, and Alexander Vertikoff, whose images grace numerous pages in this issue. We thank all the members of the ICAA staff who contributed their efforts to No. 15, particularly Mimi Bradley. We appreciate the generosity of the numerous collaborators who submitted work, offered advice, and contributed material, including Lauren Bricker, William Deveraux, Jocelyn Gibbs, Kevin Johnson, Melissa Kamen, Elizabeth Moule, Robert Ooley, Jeffrey T. Tilman, Matt Walla, and Sam Watters. Thanks finally to our sponsors and contributors to the Professional and Academic Portfolios.

Printing: Allied Printing Services, Manchester, CT

PHOTO CREDITS Front cover: Pasadena City Hall, Pasadena, California. Photograph © David Wakely Photography, Historic Renovation by Architectural Resources Group

Back cover: Casa del Herrero, Santa Barbara, California. Photo: Matt Walla

Front endpapers: Bird's-eye view of Los Angeles in 1909 by Worthington Gates (Los Angeles: Western Litho Co. and Birdseye View Publishing Co.). Source: Geography and Map Division, Library of Congress, Washington, D.C.

Pages 61, 85, 103: Fine Arts Building, Los Angeles. Photos: © 2005 Alexander Vertikoff | Vertikoff Archive

Page 104, left to right: (Downtown Los Angeles) City Hall, Central Library: Shutterstock; Union Station: © 2008 Alexander Vertikoff | Vertikoff Archive; Bradbury Building: Shutterstock; Herald Examiner

Building: Zuma Press, Inc. /Alamy Stock Photo. (Pasadena) City Hall, Central Library: Marc Appleton; Civic Auditorium: © 2005 Alexander Vertikoff | Vertikoff Archive; Caltech Atheaneum, The Huntington: Marc Appleton. (Los Feliz and Hancock Park) Griffith Park, Griffith Observatory: Shutterstock; Hancock Park Residences, United Methodist Church, El Royale: Bret Parsons. (USC and UCLA) Doheny Memorial Library, Mudd Hall of Philosophy: Shutterstock; Clark Memorial Library: Marc Appleton; Royce Hall, Powell Library: Shutterstock. (Santa Monica, Venice, and Malibu) Santa Monica City Hall: Shutterstock; Getty Villa Exterior: Photo by Alexander Vertikoff | © The J. Paul Getty Trust; Getty Villa Interior: Shutterstock; Adamson House: © 1989 Alexander Vertikoff | Vertikoff Archive; Windward Avenue Arcade: ZUMA Press, Inc./ Alamy Stock Photo.

Page 105, left to right: (Palos Verdes) Neptune Fountain: Shutterstock; Malaga Cove Plaza: Marc Appleton; Residences: Allen Creative/

Steve Allen/Alamy Stock Photo; Stables: Marc Appleton; Wayfarers Chapel: Shutterstock. (Claremont and Pomona) Tiernan Field House: © Jimfeliciano|Dreamstime.com. (Riverside, all) Marc Appleton. (San Diego) Rancho Santa Fe: Marc Appleton; Balboa Park Lily Pond, Balboa Park Botanical Building, Junipero Serra Museum: Shutterstock; La Jolla Woman's Club: Marc Appleton. (Santa Barbara) Old Mission, Arlington Theater: Marc Appleton; El Paseo: Matt Walla; Lobero Theatre: Marc Appleton; County Courthouse: Matt Walla.

Pages 104–105, bottom: Motorcycles at Venice, California, ca. 1910 (Los Angeles: West Coast Art Co.). Source: Prints and Photographs Division, Library of Congress, Washington, D.C.

Page 109: Bradbury Building, Los Angeles. Photo: © 2008 Alexander Vertikoff | Vertikoff Archive

Back endpapers: Aerial view of contemporary downtown Los Angeles. Photo: Nico Schmedemann/Shutterstock

CLASSICIST № 15
SOUTHERN CALIFORNIA

LETTER FROM THE EDITOR

Beneath Southern California's contemporary commerce and modernist development lies a significant culture of classically inspired architecture that has shaped its growth from occupation by Spanish missionaries in the eighteenth century, through Anglo settlement in the nineteenth century following the Mexican-American War, to the phenomenal economic boom during the first quarter of the twentieth century.

The flowering of classical architecture in the early twentieth century in particular had much to do with Beaux Arts–trained architects from the East and Midwest bringing their expertise to the frontier. These architects found in Southern California a freedom, supported by wealthy clients, to develop regional interpretations of European classicism influenced by the local vernacular architecture and benign weather—interpretations that were not only appropriate to the area but might lift their clients, and thereby the region's budding culture, to a more sophisticated level. What has always excited me about this classical tradition in Southern California is its colonial imperfection and regional eclecticism. It is nuanced and idiosyncratic, impacted by adventurous, ambitious, and entrepreneurial clients, by the pioneering culture that characterized the West, and by the Mediterranean climate our region enjoys.

As in much of the United States, however, the modern movement during the last half of the twentieth century was increasingly less influenced by classicism and certainly did not portend a revival in classical or traditional architecture. So fashionably persistent has modernism's impact been on architectural education in the United States that today only a small percentage of our professional schools include the study of architectural history and classical architecture as an integral part of the training of architecture students. More often than not, architectural history is not a required but an elective course in the curriculum. This is as true in Southern California as it is elsewhere. The profession has seemingly lost the facility that would allow it to speak any language other than contemporary high-tech derivatives of modernism.

When David Cohen and I naively established a Southern California Chapter of the ICAA in 2002, we therefore did not expect much interest, but the Chapter's growth has been surprisingly rapid and rewarding. Where contemporary architecture seeks to break away, traditional architecture is an accumulative experience, and perhaps we struck a chord with architects, designers, clients, and institutions for whom today's vocabulary seemed limited and/or limiting. It is important to look back as we look to the future, and this has been our Chapter's main interest: to welcome the present, but not deny the lessons of the past.

Yet classical architecture as practiced today sometimes appears to be too self-consciously academic and out of context. Without a regional context to tame and temper it, it can become as soulless and foreign as much iconoclastic contemporary architecture. We trust you will see promising signs in Southern California of the influence of our region's past on the present in this issue's Professional Portfolio.

It is a daunting assignment to try to capture in relatively few pages the rich variety of so extensive an area. Metropolitan Los Angeles is the second-largest U. S. city. Add San Diego, Long Beach, Riverside, Bakersfield, Santa Barbara, and the many other surrounding cities and communities, and it is impossible to adequately represent the classical architectural traditions that have played and continue to play an important role in our local culture. What we hope is to provide a glimpse that may serve as a catalyst for further research and exploration. I thank all of our writers and contributors for joining in this effort.

Henry Kern Residence, Beverly Hills, California, by George Washington Smith (architect) and A. E. Hanson (landscape architect), 1925–26.

Marc Appleton
Guest Editor

THE PANAMA–CALIFORNIA EXPOSITION OF 1915

MARC APPLETON

Held in San Diego in 1915, the Panama–California Exposition, like its counterpart in San Francisco, was organized to commemorate the opening of the Panama Canal. It was also conceived as an opportunity for Southern California and particularly its southernmost city, San Diego, the first U. S. port of call north of the canal, to be recognized as an important cultural destination.

In anticipation of the occasion, an impressive new railroad station, the Santa Fe Passenger Depot designed by Bakewell & Brown, was built in 1914 to receive visitors to the Exposition. The Beaux-Arts master plan for the Exposition was developed under the direction of Bertram G. Goodhue for a site in Balboa Park encompassing 1,400 acres of parkland that had been set aside by the city almost fifty years earlier.

The buildings for the Exposition were designed by a consortium of talented architects led by Goodhue and including Carleton M. Winslow Sr., William Templeton Johnson, and Frank P. Allen Jr., among others. Additional buildings were added in 1924, 1930, and 1935, many overseen by Richard Requa, a local architect who had also been involved in the original phase. Unlike those constructed for San Francisco, almost all of San Diego's Exposition buildings survive today and are still actively occupied by a number of the city's cultural institutions.

As is typical for most buildings designed for fairs, they range in architectural style and now include a number of later eclectic and modern structures, but the style of the original buildings was of a piece: together they represented one of the first influential and cohesive examples of Spanish-Mexican Colonial Revival architecture in Southern California. They were visited by thousands of tourists and had a significant impact on popularizing an architectural style that was soon to dominate the regional scene.

ABOVE Cabrillo Bridge and California Tower, 1915.

LEFT Contemporary view of the California Building and Tower, built for the Panama–California Exposition, San Diego, California, 1915.

Casa del Prado, ca. 1915.

View over Lily Pond, 1915.

BERTRAM GOODHUE
AND THE ARCHITECTURE OF CALTECH, 1915 TO 1939

STEFANOS POLYZOIDES

The California Institute of Technology—known as Caltech—is one of the most prominent science and technology universities in the world. Its campus provides a unique window into the history of California architecture and urbanism.

Caltech Before Goodhue

Caltech was launched in 1908 through a master plan for what was then the Throop Polytechnic Institute by the local architectural firm of Hunt and Grey (fig. 2). Initial suggestions by Elmer Grey for the foundation architecture of the campus reflected a classicism inspired by the local presence of the Hispanic *fábricas*, the great California civic and ecclesiastical buildings of the Colonial period (fig. 3). This Mission Revival architecture was constrained by a fragmentary approach to design that limited a comprehensive understanding of the orders, and distorted their canonical definition and application. The firm's first building on campus, the domed Throop Hall of 1910, later renamed Pasadena Hall and now demolished, is a clear illustration of this rather provincial approach (fig. 5).

In 1910, the two architects dissolved their partnership and set up separate local offices. Elmer Grey continued with Throop Polytechnic as a client. The inspiration for all of Hunt's campus planning projects was the iconic 1816 Thomas Jefferson campus design for the University of Virginia. In his definitive 1912 master plan for Caltech, and in a later project for Pomona College, most campus buildings were arrayed perpendicularly and symmetrically off and along a central axis to define grand quadrangles of various sizes and shapes. Repeating buildings were stitched together by arcades, and unique structures terminated the quads. The imprint of the University of Virginia model guided the foundation design and construction of these campuses in both the arrangement of their buildings and their open spaces. It has long since been abandoned.

Bertram Goodhue at Caltech

The architects responsible for the transformation of the Caltech campus from 1915 to 1936 were the New York–based Bertram Goodhue and his associates. Goodhue inherited the provincial campus plan of Myron Hunt and transformed it into a distinguished ensemble of academic buildings for what proved to be perhaps the most important scientific and technical learning center in our country. Goodhue was one of the most prominent and celebrated American architects in the first two decades

> The Goodhue oeuvre at Caltech is the most resolved and refined among buildings produced in Southern California during the first half of the twentieth century.

of the twentieth century. The work of Goodhue's firm on the Panama–California Exposition of 1915 in San Diego secured his enormous reputation as a classicist capable of working within the specific cultural traditions of every region of the country. His San Diego buildings, urban spaces, and landscapes were deeply Latin in form, inspired by the public and private architecture of Spain and the Spanish colonies in the Americas, particularly Mexico.

Goodhue was focused on the idea that classicism had to be specifically regional, and genuinely driven by the idea that new buildings needed to be patterned on precise knowledge of the general forms and particular details of their chosen precedents. As a prelude to his work

Fig. 1. Aerial perspective of proposed campus for the California Institute of Technology (Caltech), Pasadena, California, by Bertram Goodhue, 1916. View from the west looking east.

in Southern California, he encouraged many architecture students to travel to both Spain and Mexico to study classical and vernacular Hispanic architecture in its urban and rural settings, and to photograph, measure, and draw elements of its key residential fabric as well as its civic and ecclesiastical monuments. Goodhue wrote introductions to some of the folios that were authored and published by these students upon their return to the United States, among them Austin Whittlesey's *The Minor Ecclesiastical, Domestic, and Garden Architecture of Southern Spain* (1917). By the end of the 1920s, these published folios numbered in the dozens and today constitute one of the deepest sources of accurately documented Hispanic architecture in both Europe and the Americas.

Goodhue put these new drawings and photographs to immediate use. On the residential front, his Dater House in Montecito of 1915–18 and the Coppell House in Pasadena of 1916 (fig. 4) were the first genuinely "Hispanic fusion" buildings to be designed in Southern California. Their composition, materiality, choice of architectural elements, scale, and proportion were skillful interpretations of ideas first glimpsed in the documentary folios of his students. The influence of these two houses on the residential architecture of Southern California in the decades that followed was extraordinary. An entire generation of talented architects was inspired to follow in Goodhue's wake and produced spectacular buildings and places of their own. On the civic front, Goodhue's buildings and grounds for the 1915 Panama–California Exposition in San Diego, including the California Building, the Casa de Balboa, the Casa del Prado, and many more, were projects that could only be designed by precise reference to architectural precedents, well measured and well documented in detailed drawings (fig. 6). They consolidated the idea that the mixed Mediterranean, Anglo-American, Spanish, and Mexican cultural foundation of California deserved an architec-

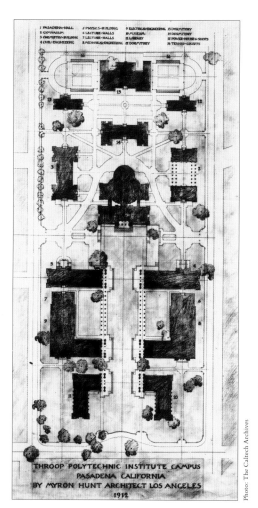

Fig. 2. Master plan for the Caltech campus by Myron Hunt, 1912.

ture to celebrate it that was authentically Latin in its derivation and essence.

It did not take long for Goodhue's approach to classicism and the architect's remarkable built work in Southern California to come to the attention of George Ellery Hale at Caltech. Hale was renowned as an astronomer, a Pasadena booster, and an aesthete in his own right. He had been instrumental in transforming Throop Polytechnic into Caltech, a national institution for engineering, scientific research, and education.

In 1915, Goodhue was invited by Hale to visit Caltech to consult on the design of the Gates Laboratory of Chemistry, then being designed by Elmer Grey. The Pasadena architect was well acquainted with Goodhue, as Hunt and Grey had served as executive architect of his first major commission in California, the James Waldron Gillespie House ("El Fureidis") in Montecito, of 1906. The sketch that Goodhue produced for the Gates Laboratory building was loosely modeled on the urban Renaissance palaces of central Spain. His choice of the flexible laboratory loft, and the building's monumental scale, with its highly ornamented central doorway and the serial composition of its ornate double windows, must have seemed extraordinary to Hale as illustrations of the potential for a new California classicism (fig. 7)—particularly when compared to the previous provincial and timid building proposals by Grey for the same building. Under pressure, the local architect eventually acknowledged the superiority of the Goodhue design and ceded the commission to him. Elmer Grey was not engaged by Caltech ever again.

In 1916, Goodhue proceeded to propose an extraordinary campus plan (fig. 8). It generally followed the Jeffersonian principles of the Hunt master plan, but it adjusted most of its building and open space features—all for the better. The plan's figural space was anchored by a large, 180-by-180-foot central quad, modeled on the

Fig. 3. Sketch for a Caltech Music Hall and Art Museum Building by Elmer Grey, 1916.

Fig. 4. Coppell House, Pasadena, by Bertram Goodhue, 1916. Front entrance.

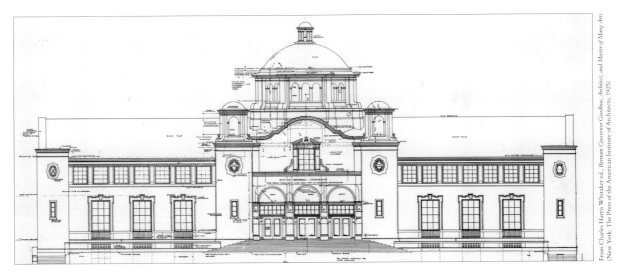

Fig. 5. Throop Hall, Caltech, by Hunt and Grey, 1910. West elevation, 1909.

Fig. 6. California Building and entrance bridge to the Panama–California Exposition, San Diego, by Bertram Goodhue, 1915.

Fig. 7. Gates Laboratory of Chemistry, Caltech, by Bertram Goodhue. Perspective sketch, 1918.

Mission San Juan Capistrano. This quad was bisected by a north-south axis that provided a formal entrance to the campus from the south. On the west side of the campus, an elegant long space inspired by the Persian gardens that Goodhue had observed and documented during his visit to Iran with James Waldron Gillespie in 1906 framed a formal entrance from the city of Pasadena into Caltech. This expanse was terminated by a domed library, the most monumental building on the campus, never built. On the east side, a large quadrangle completed the campus, enclosed on all sides by residence halls. Goodhue's perspective drawing of this east-west sequence of campus quads is the most synoptic and poetic description of the architect's intentions for the overall form of the Caltech campus (see fig. 1).

Departmental buildings were placed perpendicular to the campus edge and were generously set back and spaced apart, to minimize their effect on the surrounding neighborhood. Principal buildings such as the library and the Hunt and Grey–designed Pasadena Hall were situated perpendicular to the east-west axis, to define the three distinct campus quads. The referential nature of the main open space and landscape design for the campus, the flexible design of the lab buildings, and the formality and prominence of the most important campus buildings rendered in a novel Hispanic fusion form must have deeply impressed the school's leadership.

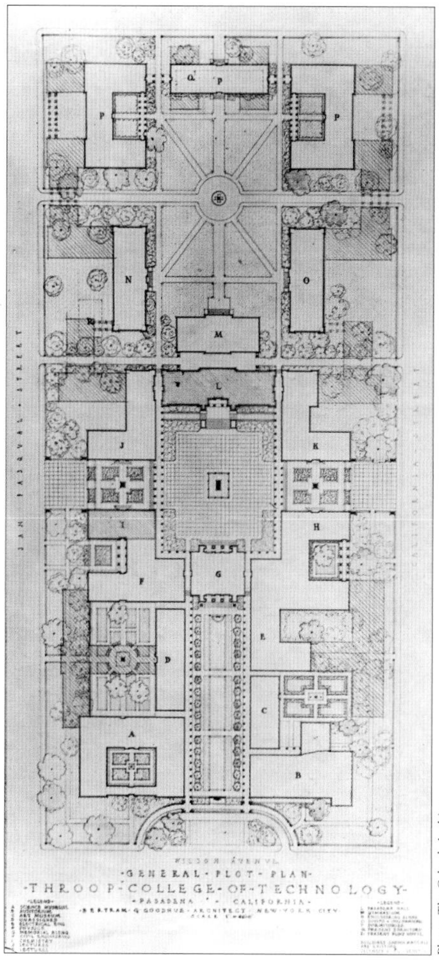

Before his untimely death in 1924, Goodhue was further entrusted with a large number of additional commissions at Caltech. Gates Laboratory was followed by Culbertson Hall of 1922 (demolished in the 1970s); the Norman Bridge Laboratory of Physics of 1922; the High Voltage Research Laboratory of 1923; and the Dabney Hall of the Humanities, completed in 1928 after the architect's death by Goodhue Associates, the immediate successor firm. Between 1929 and 1939, the entire ensemble of extraordinary buildings surrounding the western linear quad, which included Arms, Kerckhoff, and

Fig. 8. Master plan for the Caltech campus by Bertram Goodhue, 1916.

Mudd Halls, was designed by Mayers, Murray & Phillip, the New York firm into which Goodhue Associates had morphed by that time. What is unique and unusual about this last set of projects is that the design was carried out in different phases, and while they were separately constructed, they were designed and eventually realized in a singular, interconnected, and coordinated architectural form. This final post–Wall Street crash building spurt also included the most notable classical building on the campus, the Henry M. Robinson Laboratory of Astrophysics, completed in 1932.

From an architectural and urbanist perspective, the Goodhue oeuvre at Caltech is the most resolved and refined among buildings produced in Southern California during the first half of the twentieth century, the period of this region's institutional and territorial consolidation. Under Goodhue's direct influence, the firm's architecture evolved from a strict and literal application of the then recently documented Hispanic orders and ornament to an increasingly eclectic use of both European and American Colonial elements more freely composed, and finally, into a more abstract and exotic expression, representing the openness, demographic diversity, social mobility, and entrepreneurship of an emerging California culture. This formal evolution can be traced and its lessons easily absorbed, because most of the nine Goodhue building designs were cast on a common, stable, base-form, a building chassis that included several key design dimensions.

Emplacement

Caltech was founded as a distinctive scientific institution with a novel pedagogical approach. Its students were to be educated through direct involvement in experiment-based research, conducted in collaboration with their faculty. For that reason, most of the buildings designed by Goodhue were laboratories. In his 1916 master plan, these

Fig. 9. Gates Laboratory of Chemistry (now Parsons–Gates Hall of Administration), Caltech, by Bertram Goodhue, 1918.

Fig. 10. Norman Bridge Laboratory of Physics, Caltech, by Bertram Goodhue, 1922.

labs were placed on the northern and southern long edges of the campus and perpendicular to its principal east-west axis and the thoroughfares bounding it. The laboratory buildings were all of a similar size and configured in a rectangular plan. They had frontal and central entrances on the sides facing the main campus quadrangle and defined small quadrangles, courtyards, or open gardens on their rear sides. They were connected on their short ends around the main campus quadrangle with arcades.

Architectural Plan

Goodhue's laboratory buildings at Caltech were organized as two distinct plan zones. At the center of each floor was a wide, architecturally elaborate corridor, intended to be of permanent form. The plan perimeter, against the exterior walls, was divided into various rooms, classrooms, offices, and labs. The labs were designed as flexible, changeable space, finished according to the evolving experimental requirements of each faculty-student team. Amazingly, this kind of spatial organization for one of the world's premier scientific institutions has remained valid for more than one hundred years, despite constant remodeling.

Architectural Section and Elevation

The plan parti of the laboratories, and their intended flexibility of use, heavily influenced their internal spatial organization as well. They were designed as open lofts with building sections featuring a common floor-to-floor height. As a consequence of the dimensional similarity among the various lab buildings in plan and section, they shared dimensionally identical elevational planes on their short and long sides. Their resulting common massing rendered the Goodhue buildings subject to using identical structural, mechanical, electrical, and plumbing systems, which, along with similarly scaled doors and windows, entrance points, and shared ornamentation opportunities, underlined the formal affinity among them.

Construction, Materials, and Finishes

The constructional and systems technologies used in the laboratories were also advanced for their time. Buildings were produced in reinforced concrete frames with unreinforced terra-cotta tile as infill and cast stone and plaster as exterior finishes. Their electrical, mechanical, and plumbing systems were exposed within the experimental lofts. The highly detailed ornament was also produced in cast stone. Although the buildings have

been modified scores of times since, this has not substantially affected their overall form or its details.

Rhythm and Scale

Each laboratory space required doors and windows of relatively similar size. Although these were often sized differently from building to building, within individual designs they were vertically proportioned and also vertically aligned and horizontally repeated in a steady serial rhythm. In direct response to the architecture of Hispanic precedents in Spain and Mexico, buildings were accessed through a monumental stair and stoop and entered through a heavily ornamented front door located in the center of their long sides. Buildings were often folded for their entire height at their corners as a way of boosting their figural presence and, as a result, their scale.

Ornamentation

The ornamentation strategy for all the buildings focused on five features typical of the Hispanic classical tradition. These were the articulation of their mass into base, body, and top; complex framing around windows; the use of the orders to celebrate principal entrances; the embellishment of large wall panels; and the articulation of building corners.

Over the course of twenty-three years, and based on these elements, Goodhue and his associates designed all of their work at Caltech as an ensemble, a family of identifiable common forms. The buildings were located adjacent to one another, and for a quarter century, and from building to building, their physiognomy would keep transforming—from literal historicism to a lighter referential classicism and finally to a nascent modernism rooted in urbanism, historical precedence, and cultural accommodation.

The first of their buildings, the Gates Laboratory of Chemistry (now the Parsons-Gates Hall of Administration), had a dual point of departure (fig. 9). In its overall massing and composition, it was inspired by Spanish palaces of the Renaissance, while in its details it recalled the exuberant hybrid classical orders and ornamental excess of the Mexican Baroque. Goodhue's rendering of Gates Hall stunned the professorial elite at Caltech because its design was erudite. It exuded pure academic audacity, as it was based on the tangible evidence of a Hispanic classicism both American and European and was composed to specifically address the search for a new cultural identity for the American Southwest. Yet, the classicism of Gates was not radical enough for Goodhue. The building seemed hemmed in by a literal connection to its precedents, its architecture too narrowly derivative and, therefore, not the ultimate fit to accommodate and represent an emerging American scientific institution of the first order.

The buildings that followed, the Norman Bridge Laboratory of Physics of 1922 (fig. 10) and the High-Voltage Research Laboratory of 1923, were intentionally simpler. Goodhue was focused on generating an architecture that was novel, emotionally engaging, and even fashionable, at the same time being of a particular kind of classicism suited to Southern California. But what could the means be for conceptualizing such an architecture? The climate suggested that one could build more lightly here, while challenging the dividing line between indoors and outdoors. The sharp Mediterranean light of Pasadena could lead to a reduction in the depth of all ornamentation and a simplification of its profiles, as well as a shift in building coloration from gray to sand tones. Heat gain could be controlled with smaller windows, which could be thinner and lighter, as they would now be made of steel. Concrete construction could allow the design of an architecture whose durable shell was detached from the temporary nature of its interior. Reference to exotic, textile patterns could transform large, flat wall surfaces into engaging compositional tableaus. Goodhue followed through on all of these ideas and more.

The body culture of the region and its reverence for the simple elegance of the human figure, then being revealed, may have inspired the increasingly simple massing and gradual reduction in ornamentation of this new set of buildings. Their iconography remained one of Hispanic fusion, but their abstracted integration of American and European Hispanic features was becoming more evident and dominant as the original references began to recede. Digested through the filter of a brilliant traditionalist architect, the result was a classicism that blazed a relatively unfamiliar and prophetic route to a California architecture that was a bridge between continuity and innovation.

In the next and last phase of the work of Goodhue and his two successor firms at Caltech, the process of idiosyncratic design was accelerated and led to the design of two final masterpieces: the Dabney Hall of the Humanities and the Henry M. Robinson Hall of Astrophysics. These are mature designs whose architecture is both unique and fully integrated into the campus. While they are still the laboratory buildings envisioned in the Caltech master plan of 1916, their form is driven by their unique program—Dabney extending horizontally around one of the finest gardens designed by Beatrix Farrand, while Robinson is organized around the vertical axis of a spectroheliograph that stretches from its sub-basement to its dome. In both buildings, the detailing is playful and original yet still fully identifiable within the Hispanic tradition.

At Dabney (fig. 11), the body of the building emerges as a pure form finished in plaster, devoid of any moldings and cornices wrapping it, while still well defined in the round. The building's classical details are limited to a dramatically scaled main entrance, of a discernibly Mexican pre-Hispanic design, but without any overt references to the four canonical, classical orders, or their idiomatic colonial progeny. There is also a double iron balcony on the courtyard side, attached to a fountain to generate a new kind of frontage, its components Mesoamerican in form yet transformed into a new ensemble. Exemplifying the extreme end of freer expression, the building's north doorway is reduced to a framed door, the wall behind it stripped of all ornamentation and replaced by a shower of confetti, expressed as a field of colored tiles. The building's simplicity of basic form and sparsity of detail is in tension between the intense plasticity of a Southwestern Anasazi pueblo and the flatness of Machine Age architecture. In this extraordinary project, Goodhue so commands the design traditions he is operating under that he is able to absorb them and deliver through them a thoroughly unfamiliar and deeply personal architecture.

At Robinson (fig. 12), the architecture never strays far beyond the familiar, but the freedom and exuberance with which it is conveyed are notable. The building's body is rendered as smooth as possible, and its ornamentation is limited to the few places where it is needed to express a sense of public purpose—for example, in the marking of the location of the library and the front door or the placement of the emblematic relief of the sun in front of the dome. The omission of some canonical elements of classical design, such as window frames, headers, and sills, is notable, as is the building's sand-colored, monochrome body, extended across a variety of materials including plaster, stone, and precast

Fig. 11. Dabney Hall of the Humanities, Caltech, by Goodhue Associates, 1928.

Fig. 12. Henry M. Robinson Hall of Astrophysics (now Linde + Robinson Hall for Global Environmental Science), Caltech, by Mayers, Murray & Phillip, 1932.

concrete. This is a building designed at the cusp of a fully referential and a freer expression.

Bertram Goodhue and a California Classicism of Its Place and Time

Goodhue's work at Caltech challenges the current impulse of traditionalists to remain constrained by strictly normative and referential design. It advances the prospect that the mastery of the classical language, the control of the means of its construction, and its artful insertion into particular urban settings, climates, and cultures can lead to novel results—as seen in an architecture that is freer, more inventive, and more relevant in linking what we have known through the ages to that which remains yet to be discovered.

The nine Caltech campus buildings by Goodhue, his associates, and successor firms, constitute one of the finest illustrations of twentieth-century placemaking, built according to a regionalist classical architectural aesthetic. They are also a unique contribution to the ongoing debate about the prospect of projecting many regional classicisms that can be an expression of both their time and their place (fig. 13).

For an architecture to be of its place, it needs to embody some key formal dimensions. It must play a part in the incremental physical construction of the city, and its program must be tailored to the society it serves. In this architectural ideal, its types are adapted to the climate of its region, its form leverages the public realm, its symbolism reflects the nature of the culture that sponsors it and uses it, and its longevity is secured by durable materials and construction.

Fig. 13 Aerial view of the Caltech campus, ca. 1935.

Photo: John Maxon, The Caltech Archives

For the same architecture to also be of its time, it needs to respond to the evolving ethical imperatives that enable and guide the life of the society it is built to support. It must be resource-efficient, not wasteful, labor- not capital-intensive, of benefit to society at large, not just a privileged few. It needs to be flexible and reusable, not disposable. Both conserving of received knowledge and innovative, such an architecture must be nuanced in its application across a wide range of urban and rural contexts, rather than diagrammatic and stereotypical.

In the current state of a resurgent classicism, it is important that we traditionalists not focus solely on reinventing a singular American classical and vernacular culture but also that we rediscover the many regional design traditions that were triumphant before the crash of 1929 and which are such vital examples of a living and evolving traditional architecture and urbanism. By learning from these rich projects and practices, and by then operating in their spirit, we can work to secure beautiful, civilized, and sustainable built environments everywhere and for all. Both the inspiration and the process of design and construction that can be divined from Bertram Goodhue's work at Caltech provide a valuable and time-tested path for today's Southern California architecture to follow.

Stefanos Polyzoides was born and educated in Athens, Greece, and earned a B.A. and an M.Arch. degree in architecture and planning from Princeton University. His career has engaged a broad span of architecture and urbanism, its history, theory, education, and design. He is a co-founder of the Congress for the New Urbanism and, with his wife, Elizabeth Moule, a partner in Moule & Polyzoides, the Pasadena, California–based practice he co-founded in 1990. From 1972 until 1997, he was an Associate Professor of Architecture at the University of Southern California.

SOUTHERN CALIFORNIA'S AMERICAN RIVIERA

SPANISH-MEDITERRANEAN RESIDENTIAL ARCHITECTURE, 1920s–1930s

BRET PARSONS

For much of the late nineteenth century and into the twentieth, Southern California found itself suffering from something of an inferiority complex because of its lack of a recognizable and appropriate architectural identity. The rise of regionalism across the country was taking hold as each part of the nation embraced and celebrated what it deemed to be its "own" style, one that could be immediately identified with a particular place. Southern California, it appeared, had no such indigenous style but was cobbled together by importations from a dizzying variety of far-flung sources.

Red Tile Romance

Yet, there was indeed such a style, and when it made its appearance beginning in the mid-1910s it would sweep across the region in a way that could scarcely be overdramatized. As David Gebhard writes in his 1964 book on the legendary architect George Washington Smith, "In the twentieth-century American architectural scene, there has been only one brief period of time and only one restricted geographic area in which there existed anything approaching a unanimity of architectural form. This was the period, from approximately 1920 through the early 1930s, when the Spanish Colonial or the Mediterranean Revival was virtually the accepted norm in Southern California."[1]

In the Footsteps of the Padres

Southern California's enduring association with Spanish Colonial architecture began on July 16, 1769,

Fig. 1. Detail of Ford Residence, Ojai, California, by Paul Revere Williams, 1927.

on a windswept hillside overlooking the San Diego River Valley. On that hot summer's day, Padre Junípero Serra, standing before a hastily erected wooden cross, dedicated the first of what would ultimately be a chain of twenty-one Franciscan missions running from San Diego to Sonoma in the Spanish colonial province of Alta California (fig. 2).

Originally, these lonely outposts were little more than crude, thatch-roofed shanties, but over time they were replaced by structures of considerable substance. The mission padres strove to recreate in this new land

. . . the much-desired integration of indoor-outdoor living, with garden spaces becoming an essential part of each design.

the familiar Franciscan architecture of their native Spain and of colonial Mexico where they had formerly labored.

This same building pattern was carried over into the domestic architecture of the province both in the presidio towns and on the ranchos of the Spanish and later Mexican land grants. As a rule, the early adobes of Alta California were extremely primitive in design. It would not be until well after Mexico gained its independence from Spain in 1821 that a critical change occurred in the development of domestic architecture in California. Ironically, this milestone came not from the original Spanish and Mexican settlers, but rather from a smattering of American immigrants

Fig. 2. Mission San Juan Capistrano, California, founded 1776.

Fig. 3. Larkin House, Monterey, California, built by Thomas O. Larkin, ca. 1835.

who began to appear in increasing numbers, particularly in and around the provincial capital of Monterey in the 1830s.

One American immigrant in particular, Thomas O. Larkin, achieved what Harold Kirker describes in his landmark 1960 study, *California's Architectural Frontier*, as having "a greater influence on California secular architecture in the first half of the nineteenth century than any other single individual."[2] Larkin sought to recreate in Mexican Monterey the type of house he remembered so fondly from his Massachusetts heritage. With the limited resources available to him, however, he was forced to blend his favored style with that of the traditional Mexican adobe.

Built between 1835 and 1837, the Larkin House (fig. 3) was groundbreaking on many levels. At its most obvious, the house stood out for being two stories in height with a hipped, rather than flat, gabled roof, and surrounded by a wraparound veranda, or *corredor*, that was both aesthetically pleasing as well as practical. These elements, commonplace in American houses of the day, were all seen on the West Coast for the very first time, and the result was a sensation. The Larkin House was so well received that similar copies began to spring up throughout Monterey to such a degree that it begat a new architectural style known as Monterey Colonial.

California's annexation to the United States and the epochal flood of immigration resulting from the

discovery of gold at Sutter's Mill all but put an end to the gracious lifestyle of the late Mexican period. The old missions and adobe houses were left largely to rot, with many slowly melting back into the soil from which they were born.

From the 1850s through much of the rest of the nineteenth century, California began a dramatic transformation. A second "gold rush" was in tourism and land speculation, particularly around Los Angeles and the southern counties. The impetus had been the coming of the railroads, which had gone on an unprecedented campaign to boost ridership by touting the wonders of Southern California. The railroads' methods were often audacious and sometimes shameless, but they were successful for no better reason than the claims were true. Southern California's climate and scenic beauty were as advertised, and even at this early stage comparisons were being made between the Southland and the sunny Mediterranean.

During this period, many tourists were so impressed by the wonders they saw that they decided to relocate and settle permanently in this gentle frontier. Between 1870 and 1900, the population of Los Angeles alone increased from 5,728 to 102,479 residents. Just as their predecessors had done, these new settlers brought the architecture that was familiar from their former homes, and over the remainder of the century the state worked its way through every East Coast fad of the late Victorian period—

from Stick to Queen Anne. The end result was that, were it not for the palm trees, cities like Los Angeles might just as well have been mistaken for Cincinnati or Saint Louis.

This incongruity did not go unnoticed. Beginning in the 1880s, a growing movement of architects such as San Francisco's Willis Polk and other like-minded individuals began advocating for an architectural style that was appropriate to the state from both a climatic and a historical standpoint.

These efforts received an important boost from a newfound interest in California's Spanish and Mexican past. What was a spark turned into a full-fledged conflagration with the publication of Helen Hunt Jackson's *Ramona* in 1884. Jackson had written her novel as a social protest, hoping to raise awareness of the plight of Southern California's Mission Indians, but the book's noble message went largely unheard by readers who were instead entranced by the old California setting and romantic tales of the Spanish and Mexican periods. *Ramona* became a runaway bestseller, going into 135 printings and taking its place as the most widely read novel of its time. Much of what Jackson had written was highly imaginative, but readers took it as pure fact and the mythologizing of Southern California's Spanish and Mexican past had begun.

While the book itself might not have been solely responsible, it was at this same time that a new style, which also drew inspiration from the old Spanish and Mexican days, began to appear. This was dubbed the Mission Revival style. Although it was only loosely

Fig. 4. Entrance to La Casa de las Campanas, or House of the Bells (Mead House), 1927, Los Angeles (Hancock Park), California, designed by Lester Scherer, as seen in a painting by Jonathan Myles-Lea (2015).

Photo: Bret Parsons. Collection of Bret Parsons

based on the architecture of the old missions, certain signature elements, particularly in the hands of skilled architects such as Sumner P. Hunt, Lester S. Moore, and Arthur B. Benton, helped to evoke the same kind of romanticized mythology of a noble and glorious California past as found in the pages of *Ramona*.

The style, which began to flourish in the 1890s, was adopted by the Santa Fe Railroad for many of its western depots and lent itself well to public buildings and grand hotels. To some, it appeared that Mission Revival was the answer to the elusive search for an architecture that could truly be considered Californian. The style's limitations soon became apparent, however, particularly when applied to domestic use. With rare exceptions, the Mission style simply proved too boxy, with its defining elements too specific and self-conscious to be successful for residential architecture.

By 1910, the vogue for Mission Revival had largely run its course, and advocates continued their explorations in quest of a style that would accurately reflect the geography, history, and lifestyle of Southern California. The answer was nearly within reach.

The Right Fit in the Right Place at the Right Time

On New Year's Day in 1915, the Panama–California Exposition opened to great public fanfare from its hilltop setting in San Diego's expansive Balboa Park. Laid out over 640 acres, the fair was intended to celebrate the completion of the Panama

Fig. 5. Ford Residence, Ojai, California, by Paul Revere Williams, 1927.

Canal and underscore San Diego's newfound importance as the first U. S. port of call for ships traveling westward through the canal. While the fair's aim was to honor a history-making event, it ultimately made history itself by helping to set in motion an architectural movement that would sweep across Southern California and come to define the very look of the entire region.

Credit for this groundbreaking moment belongs to the renowned New York architect Bertram Grosvenor Goodhue (1869–1924). The Exposition's organizers wanted the buildings at the fair to serve as physical representations of the spirit of California and its rich colonial past. As such, they were prepared to once again dip into the all-too-familiar well of Mission Revival. Goodhue, in his capacity as the Exposition's chief architect, managed to convince the organizers to try something different, something that would still achieve the desired purpose but in a more artistic and distinct fashion. He believed that the designs should be drawn not from the California missions, but reach even further back to their inspirations in Mexico and Spain.

The buildings, both permanent and temporary,

would bring together the finest elements of Spanish Baroque and Spanish Renaissance architecture, with broad expanses of shimmering white walls punctuated by extravagant Churrigueresque decoration, intermingled with colorful Islamic-inspired details. The fusion of these compatible elements, as well as others from across the Iberian Peninsula, colonial Mexico, and California, became the new core of the Spanish Colonial Revival style.

Contrary to popular belief, the Exposition was not the debut of Spanish Colonial Revival, but the style had never before been shown to greater effect in a single venue and to as wide an audience. Its influence could be felt across the country, particularly in regions that had Spanish pasts, such as Florida, Texas, and the American Southwest. Yet nowhere did it resonate more soundly than in Southern California.

Stirrings had begun earlier in the century when a few far-thinking architects recognized the obvious connections between the topography and climate of Southern California and that of southern Spain and the Mediterranean. The similarities were also not lost on the contingent of well-heeled and well-trav-

Fig. 6. Casa del Herrero (House of the Blacksmith), Montecito, California, by George Washington Smith, 1925.

eled visitors from the East and Midwest who began wintering in the region in ever-growing numbers starting in the late 1800s. The area surrounding Santa Barbara in particular was such a match it was soon dubbed the "American Riviera."

It was therefore inevitable that the region's architecture began to reflect the Spanish and Mediterranean influence. Interestingly, it had been Goodhue who created one of the most noteworthy early efforts in Southern California with his groundbreaking design of El Fureidis, the Montecito estate of James Waldron Gillespie, in 1906. Both El Fureidis and Goodhue's later design of Días Felices, in 1915, mixed various Spanish and Mediterranean elements together to form a pleasing hybrid. This became one of the most appealing aspects of the Spanish-Mediterranean Revival style as it allowed a wide flexibility in the creation of designs that, while sharing many of the same attributes, such as courtyards, tile roofs, and stucco walls, remained wholly unique in their individual treatments. And unlike Mission Revival, Spanish-Mediterranean Revival worked beautifully in residential design of all sizes and types, from flat parcels to steep hillsides.

It also fulfilled the much-desired integration of indoor-outdoor living, with garden spaces becoming an essential part of each design. Architecturally, Spanish-Mediterranean Revival offered countless opportunities for connecting residents to the outdoors through loggias, balconies, patios, and terraces, so that gardens could be more than merely something admired from a window.

While the Spanish-Mediterranean Revival began to take hold around the time of the Exposition, it kicked into high gear after the end of World War I. The economy of the Southland was booming, and an unprecedented rise in the population prompted a great demand in building. Fortuitously, the same period marked the peak of fascination for California's romantic past with a near universal desire to celebrate it in the form of an architecture that was historically evocative yet thoroughly in tune with modern needs and tastes.

Over the next quarter century, classical Spanish-Mediterranean architecture would become a unifying influence from San Diego to Santa Barbara and beyond, until the region resembled a sea of red tile roofs. During this time, it became the style of choice for whole commu-

Photo: As reproduced in *An Arcadian Landscape: The California Gardens of A. E. Hanson*, edited by David Gebhard and Sheila Lynds (Hennessey & Ingalls, 1985)

Fig. 7. Site plan for Sotto Il Monte (La Toscana), Montecito, California, by George Washington Smith, 1925.

nities, including Palos Verdes and Rancho Santa Fe. The community of Ojai redesigned its entire business district in the new mode and, after a devastating 1925 earthquake, Santa Barbara decided to rebuild exclusively in the Spanish-Mediterranean Revival style.

The Masters

The great success of the Spanish-Mediterranean Revival in Southern California from about 1920 on, owed much to the classically trained architects who recognized and embraced its possibilities. The style's heyday occurred at a rare moment when Southern California was blessed by some of the greatest architectural practitioners in the region's history. These talented architects elevated the Spanish-Mediterranean Revival from what might have been a mere passing fashion to something enduring, thanks to the timeless artistry of their designs.

Whether they came from around the country, the world, or were California natives, the finest architects of the period had almost invariably spent time outside the United States, studying prototypical European and Mediterranean architecture at its source, filling voluminous sketchbooks with ideas that could be recreated across the Southland. In their numerous designs they demonstrated the seemingly endless variations that could result from intermingling and interchanging elements from different regional models.

Among the most picturesque of all Spanish Colonial Revival designs were those inspired by the simple farmhouses of the Andalusian region of southern Spain. By no other hands was this form more perfectly executed than those of George Washington Smith (1876–1930) (figs. 6, 7). In his all-too-brief career, which spanned the years 1918 to 1930, Smith consistently produced Spanish Colonial Revival designs from Santa Barbara to Pasadena, and even as far north as Woodside, that were and continue to be revered for their simple yet powerful elegance. Justifiably, Smith was admired by his contemporaries, who witnessed him set a new bar to which to aspire.

One of those admirers was Wallace Neff (1895–1982), who, like Smith, had spent time in Europe

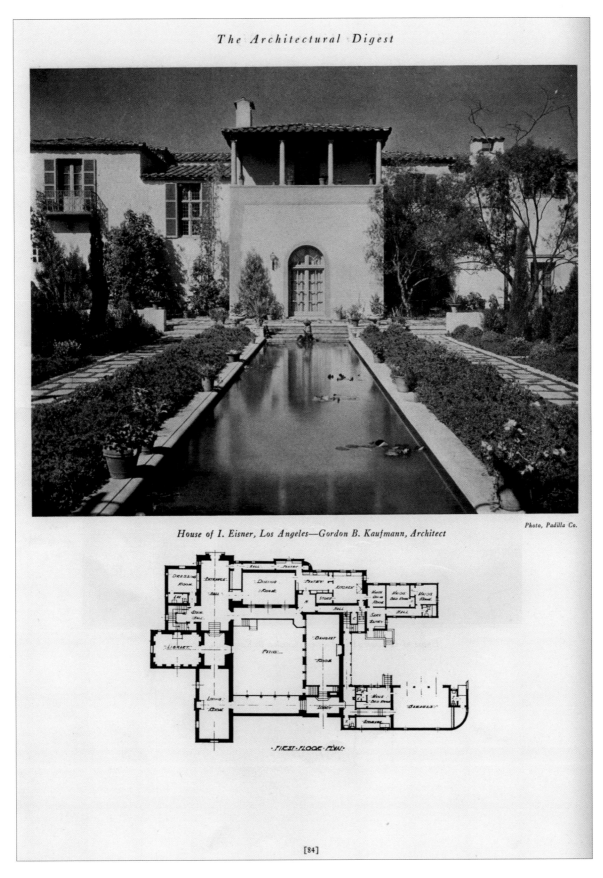

House of I. Eisner, Los Angeles—Gordon B. Kaufmann, Architect

Photo, Padilla Co.

[84]

Fig. 8. Eisner Residence, Los Angeles (Hancock Park), California, by Gordon B. Kaufmann, 1925, as seen in a 1927 issue of *Architectural Digest* (vol. 6, no. 3).

before establishing himself in Southern California as an architect. Like Smith, Neff was also a master of the Andalusian style. He excelled in various Mediterranean styles and produced notable works that incorporated elements of Spanish, Moorish, and Italianate architecture, as well as other period revivals during his long and illustrious career.

The towering figure in the annals of Southern California architecture was Reginald D. Johnson (1882–1952), who had been an early advocate of the Spanish and Mediterranean styles. He was the first Southern California architect to win national honors from the American Institute of Architects, for his acclaimed Spanish-styled John Percival Jefferson estate in Santa Barbara. Johnson's enduring contributions to the region's architectural heritage extended well beyond his exceptional designs to mentoring future masters such as Gordon B. Kaufmann (1888–1949), Roland E. Coate (1890–1952), Paul Revere Williams (1894–1980), and others (figs. 1, 5, 8, 9, 10). All three are considered to be among the most important and influential Southern California architects of their day.

Kaufmann, Coate, and Williams were all renowned for their work in variations on the Spanish-Mediterranean Revival style during the 1920s and '30s, but Coate imbued the region with a new variation through his advocacy of what he called the "Early California" house. Rather than looking to Europe or Mexico, Coate turned again to the pastoral days of early California for inspiration, seeking to recreate in a modern dwelling the same sense of picturesque romance that had enthralled the readers of *Ramona* and other such stories. Many of Coate's two-story houses were inspired by the prototypes of old Monterey and became so well-received that it started another new style, the Monterey Revival.

These masterful architects represent only a small portion of the gifted designers who worked throughout what has been called the golden age of architecture in Southern California. Other luminaries include John Byers, Lutah Maria Riggs, Gerard R. Colcord, Arthur R. Kelly, H. Roy Kelley, Robert H. Ainsworth, Walter S. and F. Pierpont Davis, John DeLario, Morgan, Walls & Clements, Lester Scherer (fig. 4), and Sumner Spaulding, each of whom left lasting contributions, both individually and collectively, to the allure of Southern California.

Fig. 9. Rossetti Residence, Los Angeles (Los Feliz), California, by Paul Revere Williams, 1928.

An Enduring Appeal

Southern California's obsession with Spanish-Mediterranean Revival architecture reached its peak in the latter part of the 1920s. By that time, the style had pervaded virtually every corner of the region and proved its adaptability from Santa Catalina Island to Death Valley. The sight of red tile roofs, palms, and orange trees set against the background of snow-capped mountains had become instantly identifiable the world over as being the "Land of Sunshine." It was a visual association so powerful it remains just as evocative of the region today as it was nearly a century ago.

While it is often thought that the beginning of the Great Depression in 1929 marked the end of the Spanish-Mediterranean era in Southern California, the style remained popular during the 1930s. It even proved adaptable to the trend toward modernism (fig. 10),

Photo: Benny Chan

Fig. 10. Blackburn Residence, 1927, Los Angeles (Los Feliz), California, by Paul Revere Williams.

which is not so surprising, considering the style's clean-lined simplicity of largely unadorned stucco walls, with minimal use of decorative elements.

Over what is now more than two centuries of architecture in Southern California, the Spanish and Mediterranean styles have retained their appeal through the comings and goings of innumerable design trends. The reason may have best been expressed by Donald R. Hannaford, who wrote in his introduction to the landmark 1931 volume *Spanish Colonial or Adobe Architecture of*

California 1800–1850, "The larger houses, and even the cottages, were built for comfort and convenience and each suits its location, showing more than anything else that what is best adapted for its purpose is the most beautiful."[3]

Bret Parsons is a realtor and founder of the architectural division at Pacific Union International in Beverly Hills, California. He has written five books, including *Colcord: Home* (2008), and co-authored monographs on the architects Gordon Kaufmann and Roland Coate. Parsons lectures extensively about notable homes and their cultural impact, and his comments regularly appear on social media and in print media across the United States.

Notes

1. David Gebhard, *George Washington Smith, 1876–1930: The Spanish Colonial Revival in California* (Santa Barbara, CA: The Art Gallery, University of California, Santa Barbara, 1964), unpaginated [3].

2. Harold Kirker, *California's Architectural Frontier: Style and Tradition in the Nineteenth Century* (San Marino, CA: The Huntington Library, 1960), 17.

3. Donald R. Hannaford, introduction, in *Spanish Colonial or Adobe Architecture of California 1800–1850*, by Donald R. Hannaford and Revel Edwards (New York: Architectural Book Publishing Co., 1931), unpaginated [xi].

MYTHOLOGIES OF THE SUBURBAN CITY BEAUTIFUL

PALOS VERDES OF THE 1920S

ELIZABETH A. LOGAN

I found myself reminded vividly of the Sorrentine Peninsula and the Amalfi Drive:
Yet the most exciting part of my vision was that this gorgeous scene was not a piece of Italy at all
but was here in America, an unspoiled sheet of paper to be written on with loving care.
—Frank Vanderlip, recalling his arrival in Palos Verdes in 1916

PALOS VERDES—Where Bad Architecture Is Eliminated.
—Myron Hunt, 1927

In 1913, Frank Vanderlip, president of New York's National City Bank, formed a syndicate that purchased 16,000 acres of the Palos Verdes Peninsula. Landscape architect and Palos Verdes master planner Frederick Law Olmsted Jr. vividly described the terrain as "a bold isolated mass, rising tier above tier" roughly 1,500 feet, complete with "cliffs which mark a projecting 'knuckle' in the coast of California at the southwest corner of the Los Angeles plain."[1] Once home to the Tongva and Chowigna peoples and subsequently portions of Juan José Domínguez's Rancho San Pedro and Juan Sepúlveda's Rancho Palos Verdes as well as the farm of Jotham Bixby, the peninsula had few residents at the turn of the twentieth century, largely Japanese and Japanese American farming families, who lived in a small handful of structures.[2] Vanderlip viewed the investment as a blank landscape on which to build and market an American Sorrento or Amalfi Coast. While the land bore histories of native, Spanish, Mexican, Japanese and Japanese American, and early Anglo American life, with farming and livestock marking the surface, unlike much of Southern California

the peninsula largely lacked layers of built construction for the new ownership to reconcile. After initial plans and setbacks, Charles Cheney, Olmsted, Myron Hunt, Kirkland Cutter, Robert Farquhar, and David Allison set out to create a "Suburban City Beautiful" on a 3,200-acre portion of the property. They privileged architecture with Mediterranean roots and enacted architectural

A 1926 pamphlet succinctly declared the development a "Suburban City Beautiful for all those who love the nearness of ocean, mountain and valley."

restrictions, the remnants of which continue to shape the city of Palos Verdes Estates to this day.[3]

This essay examines the architectural development of Palos Verdes during the mid-1920s—specifically, Myron Hunt and H. C. Chambers's home for the Olmsted family, Allison & Allison's Malaga Cove School, and E. D. Brink's Breeden Residence. Booster literature, including the Palos Verdes Homes Association's *Palos Verdes Bulletin*, championed an architectural style integrally engaged

Fig. 1. Entrance to Malaga Cove School (Allison & Allison, 1926), at the corner of Via Almar and Via Arroyo, Palos Verdes Estates, 2018.

in conversation with the climate throughout Southern California. By the late 1920s, influential architects in Palos Verdes declared "Californian Architecture" as the official style. Systematized plans for construction on a massive scale involved classifying the entire region lot by lot into three further "types" of residential construction according to stylistic qualities. Planners focused on policing design via the expertise of the commissioned Art Jury and framed the architecture as "distinctive." They defined this distinctiveness as a product of decades of architectural experimentation and maturity across California and as manifested on the scale of Palos Verdes as a planned community. At the root of their plans are foundational questions of the power to define space and architectural styles, in this case when those styles have traveled halfway around the globe and must account for decades of built realities utilizing local materials and responding to local geographic conditions. The attempt at naming a new kind of architecture illustrates the complexities of artistic expression and cultural power that practically sought to subsume preexisting categories likely in the name of both art and Anglo-Americanization. This rhetorical and architectural dance among Spanish, Mexican, Mission, Mediterranean, and "Californian" shaped spaces and possibilities for inclusion and exclusion. The actual architecture of Palos Verdes, however, reflects larger diversity

Fig. 2. Map of Palos Verdes within the larger Southland in *Capturing an Opportunity,* booster pamphlet, ca. 1923.

than planners imagined. Continuity with spaces across greater Los Angeles and the imaginative tastes and desires of owners, architects, and builders ultimately constructed this more architecturally diverse peninsula.

By 1920, more than one million people lived in the Los Angeles basin, the area newspaperman Harry Chandler championed as "Greater Southern California." Concurrently separated from emerging urban Los Angeles and part of the larger basin, Palos Verdes and its planning and early construction must be examined in conversation with scholarship on narratives of the region

during this time — Carey McWilliams's "Spanish Fantasy Past," William Deverell's "white-washed adobe" and the remaking of Los Angeles's Mexican past, and William Alexander McClung's "Anglo mythologies." This scholarship sets out the foundational cultural narration, urban planning, and lived experiences of post-statehood Los Angeles wherein Anglo Angelenos imagined and set out to create Spanish and Mexican pasts and an Anglo future for greater Los Angeles.[4]

In the specific case of Palos Verdes, planners and investors utilized both corporal and aesthetic restrictions. A 1926 pamphlet succinctly declared the development a "Suburban City Beautiful for all those who love the nearness of ocean, mountain and valley."[5] The City Beautiful movement emerged from the 1893 Chicago World's Columbian Exposition. Leaders Daniel Burnham, Olmsted, and others argued for a beneficial connection between reimagined urban aesthetics (both architecturally and to include dedicated, public, landscaped spaces) and increased public good in the midst of concerns over urban living conditions. This suburban version of the City Beautiful imagined an ideal built environment created on empty landscape rather than the reworking of an urban space in need of reform. Unsurprisingly given the era, the Suburban City Beautiful welcomed far fewer than all people, whether because of economic or racial barriers. Racial "limitations" barred the use and occupancy of persons of "African or Asiatic descent or by any person not of the white or Caucasian race" with exceptions for white families' "domestic servants, chauffeurs, or gardeners."[6]

For "white or Caucasian race" potential purchasers, community aesthetics centered on three general principles that reflect Olmsted's priorities in community planning. First, planning and construction must "preserve the fine views of ocean and mountains." Second, the natural beauty of the land must also be "enhanced with fine

Fig. 3. Frederick Law Olmsted Jr.'s house, designed by Myron Hunt and H. C. Chambers, hovering on the edge of a cliff. In the background is Malaga Cove School, designed by Allison & Allison, along the "Puerta del Norte," the north entrance to Palos Verdes, designed by Olmsted Brothers.

planting." And finally, development must ensure residents that subsequent construction by neighbors will be "an equally attractive type of building," thus preventing the depreciation of property values.[7] Encoded in building restrictions, the Art Jury, which in the 1920s included Hunt, Allison, Cheney, and Farquhar, acted as enforcer by approving, modifying, and denying proposed plans for construction. Charged with preventing "the erection, alteration or maintenance of buildings of undesirable and inharmonious design," their work demanded close attention to detail. Although specific architectural styles might be deemed desirable, a "poorly designed example of any sort of architecture, regardless of its nominal 'style' or of its cost shall be disapproved." They regulated angular rooflines and materials, ensuring, for example, that wood would not be used to imitate stone.[8]

In the mid-1920s, as part of the first attempts to realize this vision, Hunt and Chambers designed a home for the Olmsted family at 2101 Rosita Place. Hunt, famed for his work on the Pasadena Rose Bowl and The Huntington Library, designed two structures in Palos Verdes—the Olmsted house and the Malaga Cove Library at 2400 Via Campesina. The *Palos Verdes Bulletin* declared the Olmsted home the first in the community to be built hovering on the edge of a cliff, "fronting the ocean" (fig. 3).[9] Although the March–April 1925 *Bulletin* described the structure as "Spanish" architecture with a stucco exterior and tile roof, landscape historian Christine Edstrom O'Hara likens the structure to a "Mexican adobe," resembling 1830s rancho construction, even drawing comparisons to Rancho los Camulos (near Piru, California), famed for influencing Helen Hunt Jackson as she created the imagined setting of her 1884 novel *Ramona* (fig. 4).[10]

Asymmetrical and linear in design, the nine rooms stretched in a central wing approximately two hundred feet long. All the main rooms faced the ocean, captured light reflecting off the sea below, and swallowed gusts of salty air. A 1927 guest detailed the approach along "a narrow lawn bordered with flowers on either side." On the left side, Olmsted planted "a very complete collection of fruits, among them persimmons, pomegranates and figs, sapotes, cherimoyas and avocados" (fig. 5).[11]

Palos Verdes stone—a rough stone of alternately gray and orange-brown hues—accented both the structure and the landscape. Olmsted described the connection between the peninsula's terrain and the stone featured in his home: "The hills are an upthrust and contorted mass of lime-shales and kindred rocks, with a surface soil of deep and rich adobe broken by rock outcrops and with loose scatterings of the hard laminated field stone that makes such an interesting material for steps and walls and flagstones."[12]

The patio opened to the ocean, and guests (including at one point in the 1920s a class of Berkeley architectural students) rested in the shaded garden and gazed back toward Malaga Cove School. The 2101 Rosita Place of the mid-1920s captured the oceanic panorama with adobe, local stone, and the garden design of its owner, creating a landscaped Palos Verdes home—a Spanish or Mexican rancho on a Sorrentine cliff. Regrettably, much of the main structure suffered damage from cliff instability and was demolished in the mid-twentieth century.

Gazing across a ravine from the Olmsted home, Malaga Cove School dominates the corner of Via Almar and Via Arroyo (figs. 1, 6).[13] Completed in 1926, the original campus included three classrooms for instruction, an auditorium with a capacity of nearly three hundred, Principal Edith Perry's office, a faculty break room, restrooms, a kitchen, a heating plant, and acres of playground space. Architect David Allison, who trained at the University of Pennsylvania and the École des Beaux-Arts in Paris, moved to Los Angeles in 1920. David and his brother, J. E. Allison, designed, in the estimation of historian Kevin Starr, a "significant" percentage of the buildings within which multiple generations of Californians learned, prayed, worked, healed, and conducted financial transactions. Allison & Allison's notable contributions to school construction in Southern California include UCLA's Royce Hall, Santa Monica High School, as detailed by historian Sally Sims Stokes, and Malaga Cove School.[14]

Romayne Martin, a school district trustee in Palos Verdes and wife of the Olmsted firm's Farnham Martin, favored David Allison. Her preference dwelt at the intersection of student safety and aesthetics. Martin traveled across Southern California to inspect school sites. She witnessed the destructive power of the region's earthquakes and heard that an Allison & Allison school tower survived a Huntington Beach tremor while surrounding buildings designed by others crumbled.[15] Her aesthetic, as she described her decision-making in hiring Hunt to design the local library, tilted toward "Invitational" rather than "Institutional"—not an architectural style based

PALOS VERDES BULLETIN

Published by the Palos Verdes Homes Association, Palos Verdes Estates, California

VOLUME 2 MARCH 1926 NUMBER 3

Myron Hunt, Architect

ALL THE BEST TRADITIONS OF OLD CALIFORNIA ARCHITECTURE HAVE BEEN PUT INTO THIS LOVELY, SIMPLE HOUSE OF MR. AND MRS. FREDERICK LAW OLMSTED, ON THE BLUFF AT MALAGA COVE

Photo: Palos Verdes Library District Local History Collection

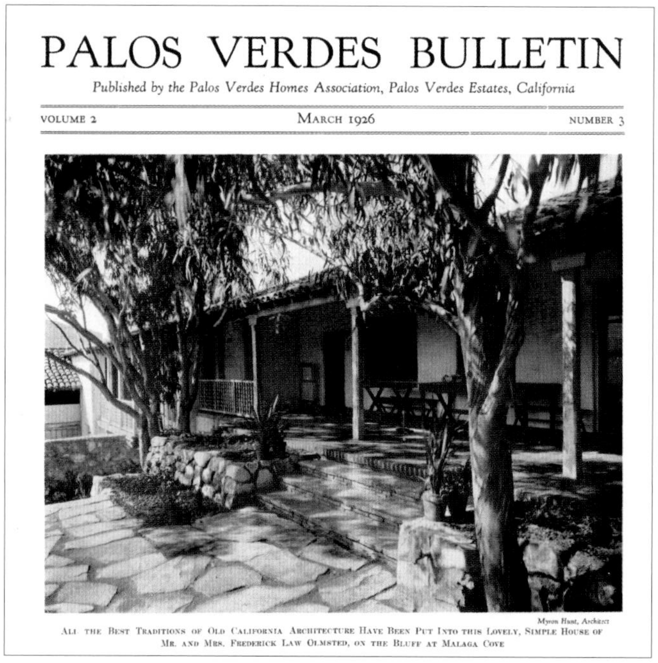

Fig. 4. Cover of *Palos Verdes Bulletin* showing porch of Olmsted home on Rosita Place, 1926.

Photo: Palos Verdes Library District Local History Collection

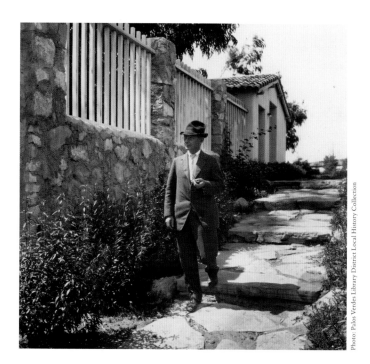

Fig. 5. Frederick Law Olmsted Jr. alongside his home in Palos Verdes.

Fig. 6. Students exiting on the Via Arroyo side of Malaga Cove School, 1926.

on an era or a region but a specific value that likely drove her selection of David Allison as well.[16]

Malaga Cove School's central building forms an L shape with a cloistered garden courtyard, planted by Martin and the first few classes of students. The axial hallways direct visitors to the space under the central tower that reaches up three stories. The most common approach to the school, however, from Malaga Cove Plaza, is a quick descent to the campus on the winding Via Almar. Thus, first views of the school are virtually bird's-eye before one reaches the building's ground level to gaze upward with vertical momentum. Exemplifying David Allison's fondness for concrete, for its creative as well as practical capabilities, the school is clad in (a sometimes blindingly) white concrete plaster and topped with a tiled roof.[17] Allison once mused, "The romance and beauty of the tile-roofed, plaster exterior building, often arched or arcaded, have had a strong appeal to all of us, and certainly this is the most distinctive style of architecture in this state, today."[18] O'Hara traces Allison's

inspiration for the school to Alcalá de Henares, near the city of Madrid, thus placing the design well within the Art Jury confines Allison helped to create.[19]

Malaga Cove School earned the Honor Award from the American Institute of Architects for "most notable school architecture in Southern California" in the mid-1920s. The design both fits within and contrasts with Progressive Era guidelines for educational built environments. The school's thick construction and contained classrooms fail to fully incorporate the open-air and open-space concept that was a favorite of Progressives and present in many other Allison & Allison projects. Heavy, wrought-iron chandeliers lit the exposed-beam ceilings of the auditorium and hardwood flooring and drew guests inward, away from the sunshine, into a distant and distinct space (fig. 7). The location of the school buildings, however, and their orientation toward the Pacific Ocean with Monterey-style balconies that welcomed breezes rushing off the water, made the school, by early twentieth-century standards, both a refuge from the elements and close enough to healthful outdoor environments for students to benefit.[20] Malaga Cove School ceased operating as a school under that name in 1991. The buildings and campus—still referred to as Malaga Cove School—currently house the school district's main office, and the district leases out portions of the campus for educational purposes. With its Spanish- and Monterey-inspired architecture, Malaga Cove School creates connections across the state with other Allison & Allison buildings. Simultaneously, the school retains its distinctive character as a bulwark that routinely smells salty and reverberates the sounds of the ocean, passing seagulls, and children.

A few blocks from the school, E. D. Brink designed the Breeden Residence at 1712 Via Aromitas for Roscoe and Molly Stark Breeden (fig. 8). Facing the ocean, the two-story house, also built in the mid-1920s, features a white stucco facade and tile roof with olive trees framing the property. Partially surrounding the ten rooms are a stone retaining wall on the ground floor and a balcony and balustrade on the second floor. Looking back at the house from the ocean side, two arches mark an entrance for guests. Notably, Aline Barnsdall, oil heiress, activist, and owner of Frank Lloyd Wright's Hollyhock House, purchased the house in the late 1920s and spent her summers there.[21] Perhaps unlike the Olmsted home and Malaga Cove School, which draw more clearly on specific rancho or Spanish designs, the Breeden Residence closely resembles the promoted "Californian" type of architecture.

By the late 1920s, Palos Verdes chose "Californian" as the official architectural type for the community, with presumptions of creating a reimagined version of the California (critically, without the "n") style of Bertram Goodhue.[22] Across the community, "Californian"-as-Mediterranean specifically required architecture to engage in a conversation with the dramatic cliffs and with the meticulously planted olive and eucalyptus trees and drought-tolerant plants purchased at the

Fig. 7. Auditorium of Malaga Cove School, 1930.

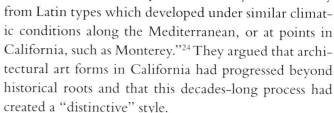

Photo: Palos Verdes Library District Local History Collection

Lunada Bay nursery. The Mediterranean architectural roots of "Californian" erased the bodies of those with more specific ethnic roots in the Mediterranean. Scant discussion of previous residents formed the narrative; one Palos Verdes promotional pamphlet, though, proclaimed it was "where once rode the Spanish Don with his rough vaqueros."[23]

Advocates of the "Californian" style across the region traced its roots to the state's past and imagined a distinctive architectural future. They declared: "California will hereafter claim as its own that distinctive style of architecture, with tile roof and light colored plaster walls, and in the romantic treatment reminiscent of Spain, Italy and the Mediterranean, which is now so general throughout the state." Surveying the contemporaneous work of various chambers of commerce, they noted that Santa Barbara, Riverside, Redondo Beach, and Glendora, among other cities, had adopted resolutions to use the term "Californian" rather than "Mission," "Spanish," or "Mediterranean." Explicitly drawing on notions of inspiration, they asserted: "Californian architecture is defined as that distinctive style which for several decades has been successfully developing in this state, deriving its chief inspiration directly or indirectly from Latin types which developed under similar climatic conditions along the Mediterranean, or at points in California, such as Monterey."[24] They argued that architectural art forms in California had progressed beyond historical roots and that this decades-long process had created a "distinctive" style.

The Palos Verdes planners and Art Jury attempted to operationalize the form by subdividing the city into residential "types." Adopting the term "type" as opposed to "style," to avoid replicating archaeological or period styles, they created three categories of residential architectural designations. Each lot within the city was assigned a type. Type I featured "Californian" architecture, which required decades of

Fig. 8. The Breeden Residence, summer home of Aline Barnsdall on Via Aromitas, designed by E. D. Brink, 1926.

Fig. 9. Samples of Type I architecture from a Palos Verdes Homes Association brochure, May 1926.

roots in California and similar climatic conditions (fig. 9). The specifications included color—to be "light in tone," with acceptable shades adjudicated on a case-by-case basis, as well as materials, including stucco, plaster, and concrete stone. A 1926 pamphlet featured the Olmsted home as an exemplar of Type I architecture. Type II houses enjoyed "greater latitude of architectural character," including English (Colonial and Georgian) and Mediterranean (modified, including Spanish, Southern French, and Italian). Lots designated Type II could contain Type II or Type I homes. Type III marked a more significant departure, including homes using clay, "steep-roofed English (Elizabethan)" and French (both Norman French and Flemish). Type III lots could contain Type III or Type II homes but not Type I dwellings.[25] The Art Jury arbitrated all prospective plans.

For Olmsted, the "distinction" of Palos Verdes rested on a harmony of uniformity with protections against a single element dangerously impairing the whole community. He praised, however, "the inventiveness and imagination of many individuals" that "must be given [a] great scope in dealing with parts, both large and small" within the confines of not disturbing community harmony "to avoid a monot-

onous and stereotyped quality."[26] The range of the three types also assisted in avoiding monotony.

It may be that Olmsted's balancing test on such a scale rendered the project virtually impossible. Or it may well be that this is what marks a distinctive "Californian" style of the early twentieth century—one that valued harmony in conversation with the City Beautiful movement, inventive creativity in dialogue with dreams of California and Los Angeles opportunity, and a high level of policing of space. The rhetorical architectural distinctions at the time among the designations Spanish, Mexican, Italian, Mediterranean, and "Californian" were at best complex and at worst arbitrary and overtly politicized. "Californian" claimed to represent progress, but it also represented the conscious framing of the state as the completed product of its previous Spanish and Mexican eras. The attempt to wash away architectural distinctions through the larger "Californian" framing is part of the process of Anglo-Americanization of the built environment. And yet, one could argue, a more effective (pushing aside normative judgments) attempt at Anglo-Americanization—particularly in a space like Palos Verdes that had relatively few structures at the time of its planning—would have had architects create a novel style that drew on neither historical Spanish- nor Mexican-California roots. In any case, "Californian," as a coherent style, seemed fragile even to those working in the late 1920s. David Allison, who helped to craft the definition of "Californian," acknowledged that some of his work, including Royce Hall, drew more heavily on "antecedents" than on this emerging framing of "Californian."[27] Notable architecture in the peninsula's first few decades (both within the 3,200-acre planned space and in the larger 16,000 acres of the peninsula) includes examples that seem more clearly tied to specific Mediterranean roots, from Armand Monaco's 1928 Italianate Haggarty Residence (now the Neighborhood Church) to the villas in Portuguese Bend, such as Villa Narcissa for Frank Vanderlip in the mid-1920s and Gordon Kaufmann's Villa Francesca in 1930. Later architectural additions, including Lloyd Wright's Wayfarers Chapel, Richard Neutra's Palos Verdes High School, and Carlton Winslow Jr.'s Pacific Unitarian Church, depart from this vision in myriad ways. While "Californian" failed to dominate the architectural vocabulary of the state, examples of buildings characterized as "Californian"—and the ongoing work of the Art Jury—powerfully connect Palos Verdes Estates' early framings to its present (figs. 10, 11).

Photo: Palos Verdes Library District Local History Collection

Fig. 10. Charles Cheney home on Via del Monte, designed by Clarence E. Howard and Cheney, who served as city planner and on the Art Jury, 1924, photographed in 1925.

Elizabeth A. Logan, J.D., Ph.D., is Associate Director of the Huntington-USC Institute on California and the West. She previously served as an Assistant Editor of *Boom: A Journal of California.* Her work explores the intersections of law, history, and culture in the nineteenth- and early twentieth-century United States and American West. She is also a graduate of Malaga Cove Intermediate School.

Notes

Thanks to William Deverell and Taryn Haydostian at the Huntington-USC Institute on California and the West, Marc Appleton, three anonymous peer reviewers, and Monique Sugimoto and David Campbell of the Palos Verdes Library District for thoughtful guidance.

The epigraphs are taken from the following sources:

Frank Vanderlip, as quoted in Bruce and Maureen Megowan, *Historic Tales from Palos Verdes and the South Bay* (Charleston, SC: The History Press, 2014), 16.

Myron Hunt, "Palos Verdes Estates, California," *Pacific Coast Architect*, April 1927, cover.

1. Frederick Law Olmsted Jr., "Palos Verdes Estates," *Landscape Architecture* 17, no. 4 (July 1927): 255.

2. For additional information on the early settlement of the Palos Verdes Peninsula by Japanese and Japanese Americans, see the 40 Families History Project, http://www.40families.org (accessed April 30, 2018).

3. The Palos Verdes Peninsula presently consists of Palos Verdes Estates, Rolling Hills, Rolling Hills Estates, and Rancho Palos Verdes. Although the original plans covered portions outside the present boundaries of Palos Verdes Estates, the Art Jury enforcement of community building standards today is limited to Palos Verdes Estates.

4. Carey McWilliams, *Southern California: An Island on the Land* (New York: Duell, Sloane & Pearce, 1946); William Deverell, *Whitewashed Adobe: The Rise of Los Angeles and the Remaking of Its Mexican Past* (Berkeley, CA: University of California Press, 2004); William Alexander McClung, *Landscapes of Desire: Anglo Mythologies of Los Angeles* (Berkeley, CA: University of California Press, 2002). Further, Olmsted's early Palos Verdes planning sheds light on his focus on creating a future Southland that marks his largely unrealized 1930 Olmsted-Bartholomew Plan. See also Kevin Starr, *Material Dreams: Southern California through the 1920s* (New York: Oxford University Press, 1991); Phoebe S. Kropp, *California Vieja: Culture and Memory in a Modern American Place* (Berkeley, CA: University of California Press, 2006); Matthew F. Bokovoy, *The San Diego World's Fairs and Southwestern Memory, 1880–1940* (Albuquerque, NM: University of New Mexico Press, 2005).

5. *The Palos Verdes of Today* (n.p., 1926), RB 81757, The Huntington Library, San Marino, California, i–ii.

6. As cited in Olmsted, "Palos Verdes Estates," 277.

7. "Community Ideals in Palos Verdes," *Palos Verdes Bulletin* (hereafter referred to as *PVB*) 1, no. 4 (February 1925): 6.

8. Olmsted, "Palos Verdes Estates," 278–79.

Photo: Elizabeth A. Logan

Fig. 11. Palos Verdes Estates in 2018.

9. "Mr. Olmsted's House," *PVB* 1, no. 5 (March–April 1925): 2–3.

10. Christine Edstrom O'Hara, "Myron Hunt and His Vision of California Architecture," *PVB* (Winter 2017): 1; Christine Edstrom O'Hara, "Ecological Planning in 1920s California: The Olmsted Brothers Design of Palos Verdes Estates," *Landscape Journal* 35, no. 2 (2016): 229.

11. "Our Gardens at Palos Verdes," *PVB* 3, no. 7 (August 1927): 1.

12. Olmsted, "Palos Verdes Estates," 256.

13. "The Malaga Cove School," *PVB* 1, no. 5 (March–April 1925): 1; "New School Complete," *PVB* 2, no. 2 (February 1926): 1.

14. As quoted in Sally Sims Stokes, "In a Climate Like Ours: The California Campuses of Allison & Allison," *California History* 84, no. 4 (Fall 2007): 27, 37; "Palos Verdes Personalities, David C. Allison, Architect, Member Palos Verdes Art Jury," *PVB* 3, no. 4 (April 1927): 4.

15. Tragically, the 1933 Long Beach earthquake proved too strong for at least one Allison & Allison school, with devastating consequences. See Stokes, "In a Climate Like Ours," 61–62.

16. Transcript of interview with Romayne Martin by Florence Sullivan, October 16, 1970, unpaginated [9, 12], Palos Verdes Library District Oral History Collection.

17. Stokes, "In a Climate Like Ours," 57.

18. Palos Verdes Art Jury, "Californian Architecture," February 1929, Palos Verdes Library District Local History Center, Architecture Box.

19. O'Hara, "Myron Hunt and His Vision of California Architecture," 3.

20. Stokes, "In a Climate Like Ours," 29.

21. See Norman M. Karasick and Dorothy K. Karasick, *The Oilman's Daughter: A Biography of Aline Barnsdall* (Encino, CA: Carleston Publishing, 1993), 101.

22. The Palos Verdes Project referenced the work of Goodhue, who was one voice in a larger conversation. See also Rexford Newcomb, *Mediterranean Domestic Architecture in the United States,* with an introduction by Marc Appleton, Acanthus Press Reprint Series, 20th Century Landmarks in Design, vol. 9 (New York: Acanthus Press, 1999; originally published 1928).

23. *The Palos Verdes of Today,* ii.

24. Palos Verdes Art Jury, "Californian Architecture."

25. Charles H. Cheney, "Palos Verdes Estates—A Model Residential Suburb," in Hunt, "Palos Verdes Estates, California," 15; "The Palos Verdes Protective Restrictions," *PVB* 4, no. 2 (February 1928): 4–5.

26. Olmsted, "Palos Verdes Estates," 262, 264, 278–79.

27. Stokes, "In a Climate Like Ours," 60.

MYRON HUNT
AT OCCIDENTAL COLLEGE

ROBERT WINTER

I first saw Occidental College in 1956. The occasion was a History Guild meeting when, as a young instructor at UCLA, I was about to be introduced to the Southern California history profession. At that time, one could drive right up to a high curb near the front of Swan Hall in the Eagle Rock neighborhood of Los Angeles where the college is located. I remember getting out of the car and, after glancing at the setting, exclaiming, "Why, this is Bowdoin College!" It was an exaggeration, but my impression had a certain truth to it. It was at Bowdoin in Brunswick, Maine, that I had my first teaching experience. It turned out to be delightful. I loved the place, but I had to admit that except for a rather awkward chapel by Richard Upjohn and a too magnificent art gallery by McKim, Mead & White, Bowdoin's architecture was basically undistinguished. Nevertheless, the lasting memory of that motley group of mainly nineteenth-century buildings was (and is) of a very beautiful campus and a lovely architectural complex. Occidental and Bowdoin, while in opposite parts of the country, have much in common—a religious founding, a small size (Occidental is a trifle bigger), and a faculty where friendships go beyond departmental boundaries. But, of course, what I was referring to at the time was the similarity of the two campuses as entities: nothing of individual greatness but everything of a piece, and the more remarkable for its contrast with the nearby environment.

The architect Myron Hunt (1868–1952) not only established the plan of the Occidental campus, but he also designed every building erected on it from 1912 until his retirement in 1940 (fig. 2). What is more, the college has preserved his buildings. Hunt was not a great architect—he was not even in the running. But he was a good architect and an extraordinarily

successful one. His more than four hundred completed buildings—schools, hospitals, banks, libraries, hotels, and many houses—testify to his ability to satisfy his clients, no mean achievement. To name buildings such as the Pasadena Public Library, the Huntington Hospital, the Rose Bowl, the First Congregational Church in Riverside, and both the Huntington Art Gallery and The Huntington Library is only to touch on the fact that he was a man of civic responsibility as well as taste (fig. 3).

Born in Sunderland, Massachusetts, Hunt was the son of a nurseryman of some prominence whose interest in gardening was to be a formative influence on the architect. He once said that landscape architecture was

> Hunt not only established the plan of the Occidental campus . . . he also designed every building erected on it from 1912 until 1940.

his favorite occupation. His family moved to Chicago when Myron was very young. Following his graduation from Lake View High School in 1888, he went on to Northwestern University for two years before transferring to the prestigious new architectural school at MIT, from which he received a degree in 1893.

Hunt married Harriette Boardman, a graduate of Smith College, and, after a long honeymoon in Europe during which Myron studied the architecture of the early Renaissance, the young couple settled in Evanston, Illinois. There, they built a house that Hunt designed in the late Queen Anne mode, labeled "Shingle Style" by the architectural historian Vincent Scully and a style that has become closely identified with the American Arts and Crafts movement. Hunt served as the Chicago

Fig. 1. Contemporary view of Thorne Hall, Occidental College, Los Angeles (Eagle Rock), California, by Myron Hunt.

Fig. 2. Aerial view of the Occidental College campus, 1938. All of the buildings on the campus were designed by Myron Hunt between 1912 and 1940.

representative of the Boston architectural firm Shepley, Rutan, and Coolidge, which had inherited the practice of H. H. Richardson, the greatest American architect of the post–Civil War period, and which later designed the new Stanford University in Richardson's style. Thus Hunt knew fine architecture firsthand and developed high standards from acknowledged precedents.[1]

Furthermore, he attracted important friends. James Gamble Rogers (who would later become the chief architect of the Yale University campus), Richard Schmidt, Hugh Garden, Howard Van Doren Shaw, and Frank Lloyd Wright (who collaborated with Hunt on at least one commission) were members of Hunt's luncheon group.[2] These close friends, along with Louis Sullivan, who was also an acquaintance, represent many of the great names in Chicago architecture at the turn of the century. Hunt was considered a valuable member of this group even by Wright, whose estimate of Hunt's importance was to become jaded over the years.[3]

Harriette Hunt's discovery that she had tuberculosis forced the couple to look for a healthier climate than that of Evanston. In 1903, they moved with their children to Pasadena, California, near Los Angeles. With his well-established Chicago reputation, Hunt had no trouble getting commissions in Los Angeles as often as in Pasadena. Perhaps that is what prompted him to locate his office in the Union Trust Building in Los Angeles rather than in the somewhat provincial Pasadena. Certainly, he was an ambitious man. Probably in order to reinforce his prestige, in 1904 he formed a partnership with his old friend Elmer Grey, who had preceded him in moving from the Midwest to California. Grey was an excellent draftsman and delineator with a tendency toward the theatrical, a trait that would eventually irritate Hunt.

Both Grey and Hunt, as former members of the Chicago Architectural Club, whose motto was "Progress before Precedent," were identified with the avant-garde, but they were, in fact, aesthetically conservative. Indeed, their conservatism was the secret of their success with businesspeople, of which Henry E. Huntington was one of the shrewdest. In addition to a hospital, library, and art gallery, Huntington also built houses for himself and for the members of his clan. Almost all of these buildings were designed by Myron Hunt and, until 1910, Elmer Grey. Reading through the letters from Hunt to Huntington (significantly there is only one from Grey) in the archives of

Fig. 3. The Huntington Library, San Marino, California, by Myron Hunt, 1920.

Fig. 4. Occidental College campus, ca. 1920.

Fig. 5. A 1909 rendering by another hand of Hunt's idea for the central administration building at Occidental College. As reproduced in the *Architectural Club Yearbook*, 1912.

The Huntington Library, one realizes why Hunt was Huntington's favorite architect. Hunt was an artist, but he was also a consummate businessman. The two men spoke the same language. The frequent letters from the firm to its client, who always seems to have been somewhere else besides San Marino, are full of the impersonal, meticulous details, mixed with a little obsequious flattery, that are the delight of the business mind. Every block of marble is accounted for and every hinge is itemized. Hunt was somebody worth paying for because he mixed art with efficiency and good sense—the client got his money's worth.[4]

His success with the business classes naturally made Hunt very attractive to college boards of trustees, first at Throop Polytechnic Institute (later the California Institute of Technology, or Caltech), then at Pomona College, and finally, when the campus was moved from its first location in Highland Park to Eagle Rock in 1912, at Occidental College (fig. 4). The business point of

view, of which Hunt was a careful student, is to get a job done in the best way possible, as soundly as possible, and with as few frills as possible. Architecturally, this philosophy does not often produce great buildings, but it does produce a great many good ones. This is the key to the fact that, while none of Occidental's buildings will ever appear in texts on architectural history, the general effect on the average viewer, including most alumni, is of a very beautiful, even distinguished campus. Boards of trustees do not generally expect great architecture. They want a campus that looks like a college but also looks as if it had been founded on common sense. This, Myron Hunt gave Occidental. The first historian of the college, Robert Glass Cleland, expressed Occidental's debt to Hunt perhaps better than he realized when he wrote in 1937, "Mr. Hunt brought to his task the ability to see both present and future needs, the wisdom to select an architectural style appropriate to the campus and its environment, and the skill to make each building add to the harmony and beauty of the whole." Cleland added, "He was also sometimes required because of budget limitations to make his bricks with very little straw."[5]

Hunt's scheme for the central building at Occidental was a remarkably beautiful design that featured a facade of two tiers of columns, the first (showing respect for the classical tradition) Doric and the second Ionic (fig. 5). A low-hipped, red tile roof topped it off. The richness of the proposed design said that it was the center of the campus, but it did not shout. Columned pergolas linking it to Fowler and Johnson Halls gave coherence to the plan. The building was still on Hunt's mind when he envisioned his "bird's-eye view" of the campus in 1913 (fig. 6). Unfortunately it was never constructed.[6]

As the bird's-eye view and other plans show, the central building, probably intended for administrative offices and classrooms, was to act as a focal point of a plan developed on a formal cross-axial arrangement with the main axis, a drive lined with trees, extending west to what is now Alumni Avenue. A minor axis would run north and south in front of Fowler and Johnson Halls, and another axis (never realized), between the next row of buildings, would march in terraces toward Campus Road and partially enclose quadrangles, at once forming discrete spaces and at the same time relating to the main axis. The landscaping was entirely Hunt's design.

The Occidental plan is obviously related to the plans

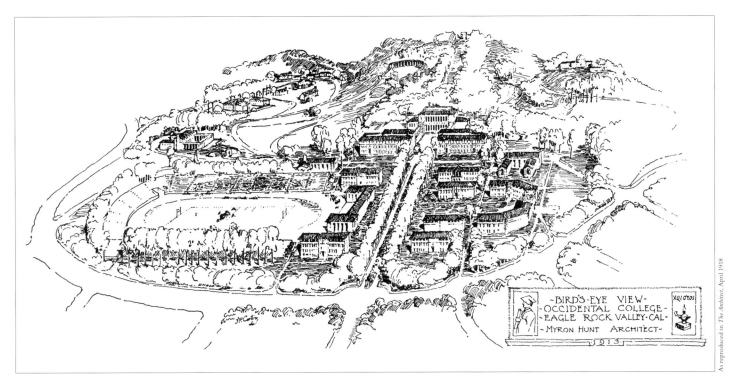

Fig. 6. "Bird's-eye view" by Myron Hunt of his plan for the campus, 1913.

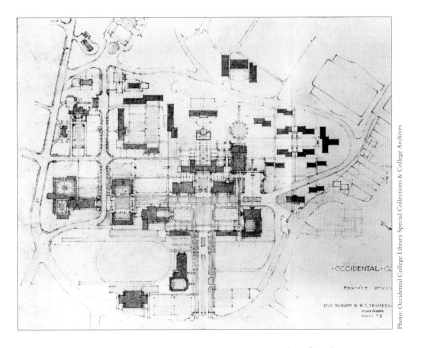

Fig. 7. Myron Hunt and H. C. Chambers's 1935 plan for the campus.

Fig. 8. Fowler Hall, designed by Hunt in 1914.

that Hunt and Grey had developed slightly earlier for Throop Polytechnic and Pomona College (fig. 7).[7] These, according to good accounts, are based on Hunt's analysis of Thomas Jefferson's plan for the University of Virginia, but the source is more clearly to be found in Hunt's training in Beaux-Arts planning that he received at MIT. Although he was in Europe in 1893, Hunt would have been familiar with the plans for the World's Columbian Exposition that opened in Chicago that year and continued into 1894. That triumph of Beaux-Arts ideas likely reinforced his earlier education in cross-axial arrangements. Similarly, he would have been well aware of the centrally planned campuses designed in the 1880s and '90s by other architects for Stanford and Columbia Universities, the University of Chicago, and the University of California at Berkeley.[8] Moreover, it is certainly no coincidence that the year 1909, when he and Grey were working on plans for Throop, Pomona, and Occidental, was also the year in which Daniel Burnham published his influential Chicago Plan based on Beaux-Arts principles.[9] In 1920, Hunt sent President Bird the famous quotation from Burnham that implored, "Make no little plans," the receipt of which Bird acknowledged with pleasure.[10]

After the dissolution of Hunt and Grey's partnership in 1910, Hunt was careful to obtain a new contract from Occidental, which was signed and sealed on January 14, 1911.[11] Other than this document, no correspondence between Hunt and the college exists until 1921, when Remsen Bird took office as president. Hunt had evidently written Bird to congratulate him on his appointment. Bird's acknowledgment promised a good relationship for the next twenty years: "I really cannot tell you how deeply I appreciate your enthusiastic support. It is one of the forces that is urging me forward in these first days. To know that you and Mrs. Hunt are back of the College means more than words can express. I like you and your way of doing things very much."[12]

Hunt learned as he built. The classroom build-

Fig. 9. Swan Hall, designed by Hunt in 1914, viewed from Patterson Field. The sleeping porches and changes in floor level indicated by the placement of windows are visible.

As reproduced in The Architect, n. d.

Fig. 10. Room and sleeping porch on the southwest corner of Swan Hall.

As reproduced in Occidental College Bulletin 31 (July–September 1914)

ings—Johnson for the liberal arts and Fowler for the sciences—were fairly conventional in their planning: each featured large rooms with tall windows giving plenty of light, and wide hallways that made for easy circulation (fig. 8). One of Hunt's few quirks was a passion for changing floor levels, a picturesque conceit that would be appreciated by Romantics but not by Rationalists. Ironically, he gave vent to his imagination most often in Fowler, the science building, where the movement of heavy equipment was mandatory and the frequent staircases a nuisance. He also applied the split level to Swan Hall, which was originally a men's dormitory divided into sections—north, middle, and south. Not only were the floors of Middle Swan several feet below those of the adjoining sections, but in addition the fronts and backs of all the sections had different floor levels. This slightly mad disposition of floors is best viewed from Patterson Field (fig. 9).

Hunt all but gave up this idiosyncrasy in later buildings. Yet he retained a more personal and important goal—the provision of a healthy environment in which to live and learn. Like many other architects trained in Victorian principles, he was obsessed with the idea of the value of fresh air and the problems of ventilation. As indicated earlier, he had special reason for this preoccupation: his wife eventually died as a result of complications from tuberculosis. This close association with disease was undoubtedly behind his becoming a nationally recognized authority on hospitals and sanitariums. But extended further, it was to make him especially sensitive to the belief that the California sun and air could not only cure diseases but prevent them. The greatest existing monument to this concern is his design for the old part of the Polytechnic Elementary School (1907) in Pasadena. With its classrooms that open by means of folding doors onto the outside campus, he pioneered the "open air school" that made it possible for teachers to take their classes into life-giving nature.

Hunt's interest in fresh air was also significant at Occidental. Among the almost hidden virtues that he designed into Swan Hall was a row of sleeping porches at the rear of the top floors of both its north and south sections (fig. 10). Clearly, at least some of Occidental's male students—it was a "boys'" dormitory—slept outside throughout the academic year. Even now that the porches have been glassed in and made into offices (I had one of them), one can experience the open look by studying the rear of Swan carefully.

The sleeping porches, also common in Southern California houses in those days, can still be seen in Hunt's later dormitories, although significantly they do not have the look of severe monastic regimen that characterizes Swan. That would be out of place in Orr and Erdman Halls, which were women's dormitories. In Haines and Wylie Halls, which Hunt designed in 1940, the porches were left out and replaced by wide verandas off the ground floors.

Many of the residents of Hunt's dormitories still comment on their livability, a result not only of amenities such as working fireplaces but, more largely, the general spaciousness of the living rooms, if not the bedrooms. Although Orr (designed in 1925, now the Weingart Center for the Liberal Arts) and Swan Halls have been remodeled, both originally had large living rooms—with fireplaces (fig. 11). Erdman maintains its spacious living room with French doors opening from a rear sun porch onto a lovely outdoor space. Indeed, Hunt's concern for gracious spaces goes beyond the design of dormitories. The "Old Union" (designed in 1928, now the Johnson Student Center

Fig. 11. Weingart Center for the Liberal Arts, originally designed by Hunt as a women's dormitory, Orr Hall, in 1925.

Fig. 12. Johnson Student Center and Freeman College Union, designed by Hunt in 1928.

and Freeman College Union), for example, with its high, beamed ceiling, and beautiful Batchelder tile drinking fountains, is a marvel of proportion. Outside is a lovely cortile with a forest of columns, the perfect place for a tea dance (fig. 12). Today, the building is so highly regarded by campus sophisticates that they prefer to patronize it rather than the prosaic "New Union."

The style remained Spanish through Hunt's involvement, with tile roofs as the unifying theme. People laugh about this Hispanicism, but it is, after all, what gives Palos Verdes Estates its character. The same is true at Occidental. The early buildings have a Beaux-Arts organization—a heavy base separated from the main mass with a lintel and then what appears to be an attic but is just another floor similarly but more emphatically separated. The later designs are looser and more picturesque in their organization, with asymmetrically placed doors and towers. Again, Weingart Center is a model.

For the new dean and comptroller's houses (now occupied by the president and dean of the faculty), of 1932, Hunt chose the balconied Monterey style, a variation on the Spanish Colonial Revival of the dormitories. The Spanish idiom was to remain constant, though watered down, until the building of Herrick Memorial Chapel by Ladd & Kelsey in 1965, which Hunt had envisioned in the 1920s as a Spanish abbey church and in a different location.

Hunt's last major design at Occidental was Thorne Hall (1936), the circumstances of whose dedication are weirdly recreated in Aldous Huxley's *After Many a Summer Dies the Swan* (figs. 1, 13). Several years ago, Professor Wellington Chan and I were walking a distinguished Chinese scholar across the campus toward lunch at the Faculty Club. As we came to the Quad, our friend looked up Hunt's minor axis to Thorne and exclaimed, "What a beautiful building!" Even though it has only one tier of columns, it alludes to Hunt's

Fig. 13. Thorne Hall in 1938, designed by Hunt in 1936.

1909 idea for a "central building." Its proportions are those admired by Andrea Palladio, although the paring away of details to almost pure geometry owes something perhaps to the modern movement. It is pure Myron Hunt, orderly, respectable, and like the early Renaissance architecture that he had studied in the 1890s, a little bit dry. The trees and the students give it life, almost as if he had willed it that way.

In 1938, as Thorne was being completed, Occidental's comptroller, Fred F. McLain, wrote to Hunt, "I frequently hear the remark from alumni and friends that this campus appears to be one that has been carefully planned. This college will ever be grateful to you for the vision which went into the original plan and has been brought to bear on this plan as changes have been introduced through the years."[14] He might have said the same about Hunt's architecture.

Robert Winter was Professor of the History of Ideas at Occidental College from 1963 until his retirement in 1994. Architecture has been one of his great passions from early on. He lives in Pasadena, and since his retirement as a teacher has continued to write. He is perhaps best known to California architects and tourists as the co-author, with his colleague the late David Gebhard, of *A Guide to Architecture in Los Angeles & Southern California*, which has appeared in multiple editions since it was first published in 1965 and is considered the definitive guidebook to the region.

Notes

1. I have taken most of the biographical details from Jean Block, "Myron Hunt in the Midwest," in *Myron Hunt, 1868–1952: The Search for a Regional Architecture*, exh. cat. (Santa Monica, CA: Hennessey & Ingalls, 1984), 9–21. I am indebted to this and other articles in the same catalogue and to the splendid exhibition at Baxter Art Gallery (California Institute of Technology) that accompanied it in 1984.

2. H. Allen Books, *The Prairie School: Frank Lloyd Wright and His Midwest Contemporaries* (Toronto: University of Toronto Press, 1972), 31.

3. Block "Myron Hunt in the Midwest," 10–11.

4. See S. N. Behrman, *Duveen* (New York: Random House, 1952), 191–217, for a hilarious account of Huntington's similar relationship to the great art dealer Joseph Duveen, who sold him Gainsborough's *Blue Boy* and many other pictures that are now in the Huntington Art Gallery in San Marino, California.

5. Robert Glass Cleland, *The History of Occidental College, 1887–1937* (Los Angeles: Ward Richie Press, 1937), 45.

6. In once describing the drawing, President Arthur G. Coons exclaimed, "Shades of old Perugia."

7. These as well as the plan for Occidental College are extensively discussed in Stefanos Polyzoides and Peter de Bretteville, "Myron Hunt as Architect of the Public Realm," in *Myron Hunt, 1868–1952*, 92–109.

8. See Paul Venable Turner, *Campus: An American Planning Tradition* (Cambridge, MA: MIT Press, 1984), esp. ch. 5, "The University as City Beautiful."

9. See esp. Thomas S. Hines, *Burnham of Chicago: Architect and Planner* (New York: Oxford University Press, 1974), 312–45.

10. Remsen Bird, letter to Myron Hunt, March 27, 1923, Letters and Papers of Remsen Bird, Occidental College Library Special Collections & College Archives (hereafter LPRB).

11. Contract between Myron Hunt and Occidental College, folder "Myron Hunt," LPRB. (This document oddly appears in the papers of Remsen Bird, president of the college from 1921 to 1946, although it was transacted during the presidency of John Willis Baer, which extended from 1906 to 1916.) Amusingly, the date that Hunt wrote after his name was "January 14, 1910." Like many of us, he had trouble catching up with the new year. The late Jean Paule, secretary of the college, checked the transaction in the minutes of the Board of Trustees and confirmed the accuracy of the 1911 date.

12. Remsen Bird, letter to Myron Hunt, August 16, 1921, LPRB.

13. In Aldous Huxley's novel *After Many a Summer Dies the Swan* (1939), Occidental appears as "Tarzana College" and President Bird as "President Mulge," although Huxley later said he intended that character to be a composite of Bird and President Rufus B. von KleinSmid of the University of Southern California. According to campus legend, Huxley, who had been considered for a professorship in Occidental's English Department, was forever exiled from the college.

14. Fred F. McLain, letter to Myron Hunt, June 20, 1938, LPRB. After 1920, the firm became Hunt & Chambers. When Hunt retired in 1940, the firm became Chambers & Hibbard and was retained by Occidental College.

CIVIC ARCHITECTURE IN SOUTHERN CALIFORNIA

PASADENA CITY HALL AND
SANTA BARBARA COUNTY COURTHOUSE

MARC APPLETON

Two memorable early twentieth-century buildings in Southern California capture this region's architectural culture and exemplify what can happen when classical aesthetic impulses settle here. The two buildings—Pasadena City Hall and the Santa Barbara County Courthouse—are both public rather than private, they were coincidentally designed by different architects from San Francisco and completed in the same year (1929), and although located in different cities, they were conceived according to the same basic planning principles, sharing a similar urban vision and scale (fig. 1).

As alike as they are in these ways, they are also remarkably different in character, style, and detail. Pasadena City Hall, designed with controlled authority by Bakewell & Brown, is a formal, symmetrical building. The Santa Barbara County Courthouse, designed more informally by William Mooser & Co., is an asymmetrical complex of four buildings. Both have heightened my appreciation of the ability of the classical language of architecture, in capable hands, to be acclimatized and successfully adapted to a specific region in ways that make the language richer.

Pasadena City Hall

Pasadena City Hall was one of several key institutional buildings proposed as part of a 1922 master plan for a new civic center in Pasadena by the planner Edward

Fig. 1. Pasadena City Hall (TOP) by Bakewell & Brown, 1927, and Santa Barbara County Courthouse (BOTTOM), by William Mooser & Co., 1929.

H. Bennett (1874–1954). Bennett, an architect as well as a planner, was educated at the École des Beaux-Arts in Paris, and with Daniel Burnham had already developed plans for San Francisco (1903) and Chicago (1909). In the spring of 1922, he was invited to visit Pasadena by George Ellery Hale, an astronomer on the faculty of Caltech who was also from Chicago, a friend of Burnham's, and had a keen interest in Pasadena's future as a city.[1] A year later, Bennett returned and presented the first plan for Pasadena's new Civic Center (fig. 2). In addition to a new city hall, the plan included a new public library and civic auditorium.

In December 1923, the City of Pasadena sponsored an invitational competition for nine architectural firms

The architecture of these buildings invites public use and participation beyond their stated functions.

to submit schemes for the three main buildings included in the plan. In February 1924, Myron Hunt was selected for the library, Edwin Bergstrom for the auditorium, and Bakewell & Brown for the City Hall commission. Bennett and his firm—Bennett, Parsons, Frost & Thomas—continued to develop the civic plan and presented a final version in 1925 that incorporated the schemes for the new buildings (fig. 3). Although Arthur Brown Jr.'s design for City Hall evolved and was refined over the next year and a half, notably and most significantly with

Fig. 2. Plan for Pasadena's Civic Center, 1923, by Bennett, Parsons, Frost & Thomas.

the original central entry Mission-style "bell wall" being replaced by a domed tower, the basic conceptual layout remained intact. As John Bakewell initially described it in a press release, "The entrance to the building is really an entrance to the patio, and from the patio one can proceed to the desired department directly. This makes the interior court an integral part of the plan, and everyone entering the building passes through the court."[2]

The building plan is rectangular and rigorously symmetrical (fig. 4). The side enclosing wings, elegantly but minimally detailed, are two stories high with alternating windows and double-height pilasters supporting an entablature, above which a third attic story sets back behind a balustraded balcony. The attic story is a continuation of the projecting and more highly decorated main entry entablature, which supports an octagonal tower that serves as an open-air belvedere. Paired Ionic columns flank arches on this level, supporting in turn a second, higher

entablature on which sit more arches and a tiled circular dome capped by a lead cupola. The tower is a magnificent and energetic pile of Baroque classical elements (fig. 5).

In initial rough sketches for the domed tower (fig. 6), Brown had considered pushing it to the center of the courtyard. In the end, however, he pulled it back to the position originally occupied by the bell wall, leaving the courtyard as the grand outdoor "patio" entry hall the architect had first envisioned and positioning the tower to front the street, commanding a more prominent presence on the civic plaza.

The extravagance of the tower's ornament can be seen as an intentional gesture. Where the principal wings of the building are straightforward and functional, the design of the domed tower takes on a more exuberant massing and detail.[3] Brown may have drawn initial inspiration from the gatehouse for the Palais de Luxembourg by Salomon de Brosse, but adapted it to his plan and amplified the detailing relative to the rest of his build-

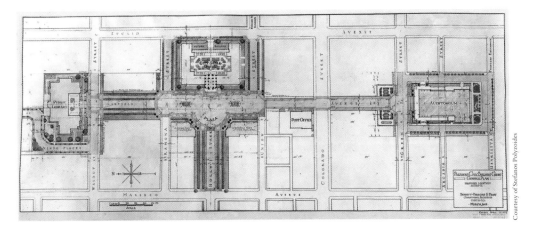

Fig. 3. Plan for Pasadena's Civic Center, 1925, by Bennett, Parsons, Frost & Thomas.

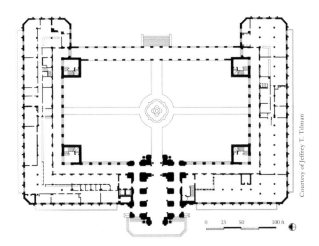

Fig. 4. Pasadena City Hall, first-floor plan, ca. 1926.

Fig. 5. Domed tower, Pasadena City Hall.

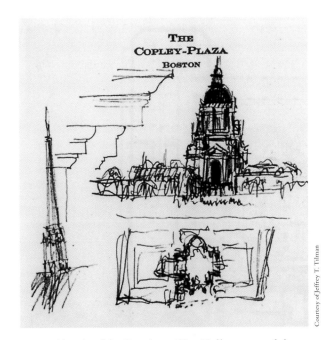

Fig. 6. Sketch of the Pasadena City Hall tower and dome by Arthur Brown Jr., ca. 1925.

Fig 7. Central courtyard fountain, Pasadena City Hall.

Fig. 8. An event in the central courtyard of the Pasadena City Hall.

ing. There was a moment during budget hearings when the city entertained eliminating the tower, but the architects prevailed, successfully arguing that to sacrifice this element of the design would mean losing the main focal point for the Civic Center.

Indeed, it is the contrasting height and ceremonial richness of the tower's architecture and decorative elements that reinforce the building's civic stature. The dome, like that of a European town's cathedral, rises at the urban core, appropriately relating government's seat to the surrounding city. The tower's architecture is a happy creation, one that Charles Moore and his co-authors of *The City Observed: Los Angeles* referred to as a "frothed-up wedding cake, full of air on the inside."[4]

The building is as open and romantic as Bakewell & Brown's earlier 1913 San Francisco City Hall is closed and formal. Entering through the grand arch at the street, one is seduced through to the courtyard by the sight of a giant tiered fountain at its center and the sounds of splashing water (fig. 7). There are no distractions of a grand stair or spacious arrival hall to break this ceremonial passage from outside on the street, through the archways, and then back outside again to the landscaped courtyard. Once in the courtyard, one's gaze is drawn to the two quadrants of eight California live oak trees, along with the grand fountain and parterres of flower beds divided by decomposed granite pathways similar to those found in a Mediterranean

garden. The four corner stair towers interconnect passageways on both floors that are arcaded open-air corridors encouraging views back to this interior landscape.

One element that did not survive the budget cuts was a rear wing containing City Council chambers and a mayoral suite that would have completely enclosed the central courtyard. A ground-level pergola was built instead, continuing the peristyle columns of the other three sides and allowing a view through the courtyard across Euclid Street to Johnson, Kaufmann & Coate's All Saints Episcopal Church of 1925.

In addition to serving as an entry to the City Hall's various agencies, the building's courtyard is a popular tourist destination and lunch spot, as well as the location for weddings and other events (fig. 8). It is a tribute to the architect and the city officials who championed the design that the City Hall so hospitably accommodates public activities and is open and inviting not only to those doing business there but to the casual visitor as well.

Santa Barbara County Courthouse

If there are aspects of Pasadena's City Hall that border on hyperbole, they would be considered mild compared to the unbridled brio and joie de vivre of the architecture of Santa Barbara's County Courthouse (fig. 9). The context in which the courthouse acquired its extraordinary character deserves some explanation.

Fig. 9. Main entry and clock tower of the Santa Barbara County Courthouse.

Fig. 10. Santa Barbara County Courthouse, Anacapa Street elevation.

Santa Barbara—like Pasadena—had its own unique vision of the City Beautiful movement. By the end of the nineteenth century, it had become an attractive resort and vacation destination, with major hotels such as the Arlington and the Potter. It had also become home to many who decided to stay and settle there, and these residents were committed to giving their city a more civilized and place-appropriate cultural identity.

They were accidently assisted by an unfortunate event: in June 1925 a devastating earthquake destroyed much of the city, including many of its government and cultural buildings as well as its grand hotels. In the aftermath of the earthquake, several concerned and powerful citizens, led by Bernard Hoffman and Pearl Chase, decided to take charge of the rebuilding of the city and determined it should have a controlled building plan that promoted a unified architectural style in the Spanish Colonial tradition. Through the newly established Plans and Planning Committee of the County Arts Association, they successfully bureaucratized the design review process. They brought in the planner Charles H. Cheney, an associate of the Olmsted Brothers firm, and also enlisted talented California architects—George Washington Smith, Carleton M. Winslow, Reginald Johnson, and others—to advise the committee and help establish the Community Drafting Room to work on specific projects.

One of the products of these efforts was the publication of *Californian Architecture in Santa Barbara*,[5] a collection of photographs of historical architectural precedents as well as contemporary Spanish Colonial and Mediterranean Revival work by local architects, including many by the same architects who were advising the committee, an act of favoritism that was easily accepted given the appropriateness of their work to the cause. The publication was a cleverly calculated guidebook for the city and county's redevelopment.

When the County Board of Supervisors commissioned the San Francisco firm of William Mooser & Co. to design a new courthouse to replace the one destroyed by the earthquake, it was under the influence of this new civic identity that the board's somewhat vague brief to the architect dictated that the new building should be "in the Spanish Style."[6] The firm selected was not particularly distinguished for its design work. The chief principal, William Mooser II, had been trained as an engineer. Yet the firm had won second place in an earlier 1919 design competition for a new county building for Santa Barbara, for which Mooser & Co. had come up with a less ambitious and more budget-conscious

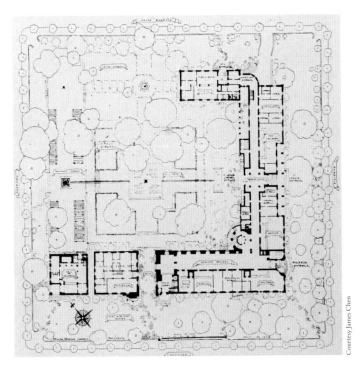

Fig. 11. Santa Barbara County Courthouse, first-floor plan from a pamphlet published by the Santa Barbara County Board of Supervisors.

scheme, and it was perhaps their more conscientious approach rather than their design reputation that led the Supervisors to choose the runner-up.

Once certain of the commission for the new courthouse, William Mooser II prevailed upon his son, William Mooser III, to join his father's firm to manage the project. The son had been trained in architecture at the École des Beaux-Arts and had traveled extensively in Europe (including Spain), and it was fortuitous that he accepted his father's offer. As the architect began to develop plans, however, there were so many conflicting points of view among all concerned regarding the program and design that the County Board of Supervisors was ultimately forced to appoint an arbitration board to try to resolve the disagreements. George A. Batchelder, a retired banker who had been instrumental in developing Santa Barbara's Riviera neighborhood, took over the leadership of the arbitration board, and asked J. Wilmer Hershey, a young architect and member of the Community Drafting Room, to make sketches for a revised scheme.

Although Mooser & Co. must have been exasperated by the process, it was to the firm's credit that it accepted this intrusive input cooperatively and graciously, and the design evolved toward general approval and acceptance. Hershey's suggestions encouraged a less formal

and more romantic character, reflecting elements from southern Spain and Andalusia rather than more formal Spanish Renaissance buildings of cities like Madrid. Hershey unfortunately became ill and died at the age of thirty-one, but Mooser & Co. developed the design to finished plans incorporating many of Hershey's ideas.

Budget constraints had also affected the design, and adopting a more informal, vaguely southern Spanish vocabulary of materials and finishes was consistent with this. Cement plaster, ceramic tile, local stone, and wrought iron were certainly less expensive than marble or bronze, and they were more compatible with the looser architectural style. In addition, the County Board of Supervisors was not entirely committed to handing the construction over to a large corporate general contractor but chose instead to bid out different parts and pieces to local contractors and subcontractors, who added their own input to the final design and details.

One can speculate to what extent the architectural outcome was affected, not only by the choice of an architect willing to entertain input from others but also by the vicissitudes of the program, design, and construction process. As it evolved, the building became a grand but vernacular Spanish *palacio* on steroids. It was, in the end, overscaled but also approachable. Held together by a consistency of materials, the building is a potpourri of disparate elements that delight the eye (fig. 10). Charles Moore described the courthouse as "a confection that is like many things, but accurate to nothing"[7] and called it "one of the century's great monuments to the architecture of inclusion."[8] It seems that no architectural detail was too irrelevant but would find a place somewhere in the mix. One suspects that if the ceramic tile or wrought iron subcontractor had an idea, somehow the architect had willingly considered it. The ensuing whimsical and enthusiastic medley of details is irrational but irresistibly inviting.

The fact that the building was programmatically an accommodation of four separate government buildings—the Hall of Records, Main Administration and Courts, Service Annex, and Jail—no doubt contributed to the disjointed but picturesque result (fig. 11). Between the Hall of Records and the Main Administration and Courts is a monumental ceremonial entry archway, eccentrically accented by a clock and observation tower. The archway is supported on one side by a column that sits classically on a base, and on

Fig. 12. Main entry arch of the Santa Barbara County Courthouse from Anacapa Street.

Fig. 13. Figueroa Street entry ("Lawyers Entrance") of the Santa Barbara County Courthouse.

the other by a column that seems to engage part of some abstract quarry of stone blocks cascading into a fountain (fig. 12). This grand entry—like that of Pasadena City Hall's—does not lead into the building but, rather, *through* it to a central, parklike courtyard with a spectacular view of trees and the surrounding mountains. Off to the right side, almost as an afterthought, is the actual but more diminutive pedestrian entrance to the Main Administration and Courts building.

The irony of this gesture occurs elsewhere throughout the complex, such as in the grand southeast circular stair tower, where the stair actually contracts to a dead end as it ascends, leading nowhere. At the "Lawyer's Entrance," near the corner of Anacapa and Figueroa Streets (fig. 13), is a multiframed stone archway bearing the inscription "Reason Is the Life of the Law" that resembles a grand entrance to some neo-Gothic cathedral. The actual doorway, however, is proportionally too small and has been squeezed way off-center to the right. Reason may be the life of the law, but not of the architecture!

Touring the building, one is bombarded everywhere by nonsensical but serendipitous architectural gestures and details. This is architecture where Vitruvian delight has, to be sure, overwhelmed commodity and firmness. On the great overscaled loggia of the second floor of the Main Courts wing, the thick sills at the openings defy logic and are too high for one to lean on and look over into the courtyard below, but low enough to appreciate the trees, mountains, and sky. A quatrefoil window is centered above the grand entry arch, but off-center on the eccentric gabled roof above. The fenestration

Fig. 14. Jail wing, Santa Barbara County Courthouse, viewed from the garden courtyard.

of the Jail wing is a lively but contradictory array of different openings and elements composed for the amusement of the public, one suspects, rather than the hapless inmates (fig. 14). The list of unexpected vignettes goes on.

From the day of its inauguration, the Santa Barbara County Courthouse welcomed public use (fig. 15). It was officially dedicated August 14, 1929, the opening day of Santa Barbara's annual Old Spanish Days Fiesta, and it has played host to the fiesta and other public ceremonies and events ever since. Local organizations take advantage of its landscaped courtyard and corridors for fund-raisers and dinner parties, and the Mural Room, which was for many years the County Board of Supervisors' assembly room, is now the setting for receptions and weddings when it is not being visited by tourists admiring the impres-

Fig. 15. Ruiz-Botello Pageant during one of the early celebrations of the Old Spanish Days Fiesta at the Santa Barbara County Courthouse.

Fig. 16. Mural Room, Santa Barbara County Courthouse.

sive murals depicting a romanticized early history of Santa Barbara (fig. 16).[9]

Buildings That Belong

Responding sensitively to a unique circumstance, time, and place, Pasadena City Hall and the Santa Barbara County Courthouse represent the enduring appeal of such additions to the urban fabric. They truly *belong* to their cities. Both of these buildings are products of classical provenance. Neither, however, was conceived "by the book" or according to any strict classical formula or precedent. They were forged idiosyncratically in their particular locales, each affected in distinct ways by program, climate, and—last but not least—by a planning and architectural design process that considered them as part of, not separate from, the larger context of the city's identity.

In each case, it seems that those in charge were eager to create buildings that were of public as well as private use and benefit. What resulted was of a place and part of a particular urban context. The architecture of these buildings invites public use and participation beyond their stated functions. They are welcoming and inclusive. To enter and experience them is to be reminded of where they are: in a part of the country and a climate where inside and outside are inextricably interconnected.

In an essay for an issue of the *Classicist* devoted to New York, Allan Greenberg remarked, "Lacking a vision of urbanism, most of today's architects prefer to present their buildings as isolated events rather than as part of a greater whole."[10] Southern California is, to be sure, of a very different urban density and scale than New York—horizontal rather than vertical—but the last half century of iconoclastic architectural additions to western cities makes this criticism just as applicable to our region. The two civic buildings remembered here present a convincing argument against isolated, self-centered designs and in favor of more public-spirited and inclusive solutions. They are as loved today as they were when first constructed.

A native of California and Arizona, **Marc Appleton** is the founding principal of Appleton Partners LLP, with offices in Santa Monica and Santa Barbara, California. He received a B.A. in English from Harvard College (1968) and an M.Arch. degree from the Yale School of Architecture (1972). His design work has received many awards and has been widely published, and he has also written and published numerous books, most recently, *Ranches: Home on the Range in California* (Rizzoli International Publications, 2016).

Notes

1. Hale was typical of many of his fellow Pasadenans who were "partisans of cultural uplift." See David Gebhard and Robert Winter, *Architecture in Los Angeles* (Salt Lake City: Gibbs Smith, 1985), 338.

2. As quoted in Jeffrey T. Tilman, *Arthur Brown Jr.: Progressive Classicist* (New York: W. W. Norton, 2006), 138. Tilman's book contains one of the most complete histories of Pasadena City Hall; see pages 135–43.

3. Tilman, *Arthur Brown Jr.*, 140.

4. Charles Moore, Peter Becker, and Regula Campbell, *Los Angeles: The City Observed* (New York: Vintage Books, 1984), 328.

5. H. Phillip Staats, ed., *Californian Architecture in Santa Barbara* (New York: Architectural Book Publishing Co., 1929; repr. 1990).

6. Patricia Gebhard and Kathryn Mason, *The Santa Barbara County Courthouse* (Santa Barbara, CA: Daniel & Daniel Publishers, 2001), 17–18. This is the only publication on the general history of the Santa Barbara County Courthouse.

7. Charles Moore and Gerald Allen, *Dimensions* (New York: Architectural Record Books, 1976), 41–50.

8. Charles Moore, "Plug It in, Rameses, and See if It Lights up. Because We Aren't Going to Keep It Unless It Works," *Perspecta* 11, (1967): 42.

9. The murals were painted by Dan Sayre Groesbeck, an illustrator, billboard painter, and self-taught artist.

10. Allan Greenberg, "Into the Looking Glass," in *Classicist* 14 (New York: Institute of Classical Architecture & Art, 2017), 59.

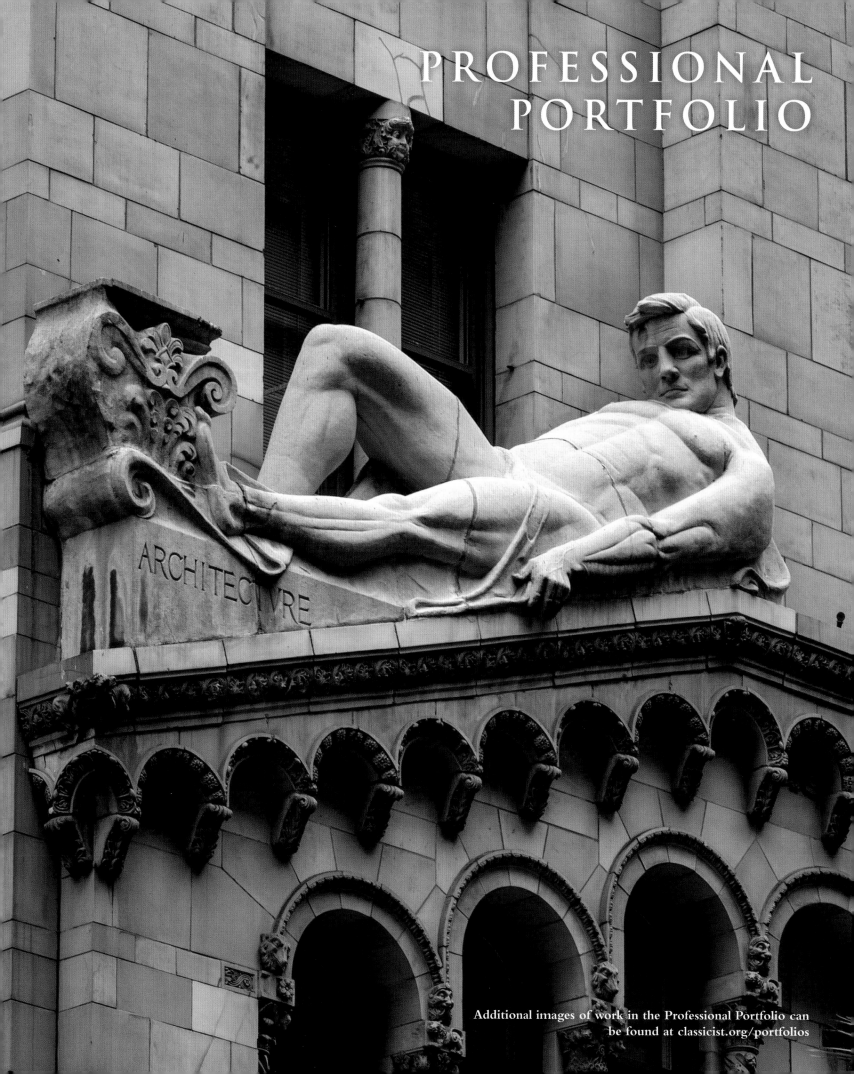

PROFESSIONAL PORTFOLIO

ARCHITECTVRE

Additional images of work in the Professional Portfolio can
be found at classicist.org/portfolios

Residence, Brentwood, Los Angeles
Ferguson & Shamamian Architects   Landscape: Mia Lehrer & Associates

Villa Vittoria, Beverly Hills
Thomas Proctor Architect

Maison Dunand, Beverly Hills
Richard Manion Architecture   Landscape: Leyva Wilde

Villa Due Palme, Beverly Hills
Thomas Proctor Architect

Villa, Beverly Hills
Kevin A. Clark Inc., Architect   Landscape: EPT Design/Nord Eriksson

Photo: Hester + Hardaway Photography

Residence, La Cañada Flintridge
Michael Burch Architects

Photo: Thomas Bollay

Palacio de la Vista, Montecito
Thomas Bollay Architects, Inc.   Landscape: Eric Nagelmann

Photo: Matt Walla

Florestal Pool House, Santa Barbara
Appleton Partners LLP   Landscape: Appleton Partners LLP

Hacienda de la Paz, Los Angeles
Rafael Manzano Martos   Landscape: Rafael Manzano Martos   Client, Developer, and Builder: John Z. Blazevich

Photo: Werner Segarra Photography

Residence, Rancho Santa Fe
Island Architects   Landscape: TCLA Studio

Photo: John Ellis

Residence, Malibu
Lewin Wertheimer, Architect   Landscape: Marny Randall

Family Compound, Encinal Bluffs, Malibu
Robert A.M. Stern Architects   Landscape: Deborah Nevins & Associates

Quail H Ranch, Santa Ynez Valley
Appleton Partners LLP   Landscape: Appleton Partners LLP

Photo: Jim Bartsch

Rancho San Miguel, Santa Barbara
Jeff Shelton, Architect   Landscape: Jeff Shelton

Photo: Lepere Studio

Rancho San Leandro, Montecito
Tom Meaney Architect

Photo: Tim Street-Porter

Photo: Tim Street-Porter

French Ranch, Hidden Valley
Michael Burch Architects and Thomas Bollay Architects, Inc.

Plaza la Reina, Hotel and Retail, Westwood, Los Angeles
Moule & Polyzoides Architects and Urbanists

Photo: Karin Shelton

Photo: Wayne McCall

El Andaluz, Apartments and Commercial, Santa Barbara
Jeff Shelton, Architect

Photo: Emmalee Thomas

Casas Las Granadas, Multi-family Affordable Housing, Santa Barbara
RRM Design Group   Landscape: Sliding Design

Photo: Jim Bartsch

Paseo Bonito, Multi-family Housing, Santa Barbara
The Cearnal Collective   Landscape: David Black & Associates

Photo: Jim Bartsch

Chapala One, Mixed Use, Santa Barbara
DesignARC, Inc.

Our Savior Church and USC Caruso Catholic Center, Los Angeles
Elkus Manfredi Architects   Architect of Record: Perkowitz + Ruth

Our Lady of the Most Holy Trinity Chapel, Thomas Aquinas College, Santa Paula
Duncan Stroik Architect   Architect of Record: Rasmussen and Associates

Photo: Jim Bartsch

1100 Santa Barbara Street, Commercial, Santa Barbara
DMHA Architecture + Interior Design   Landscape: Arcadia Studio

Photo: A New Medley Photography

Santa Barbara Bank & Trust, Santa Barbara
The Cearnal Collective   Landscape: Arcadia Studio

Hotel Californian, Mixed Use, Santa Barbara
DesignARC, Inc.

Granada Garage and Office Building, Santa Barbara
Architect, Engineer, and Parking Planner: Watry Design Inc.   Design Architect: Henry Lenny Design

Jungels–Winkler Residence Hall, Scripps College, Claremont
BAR Architects   Landscape: SWA Group

Conrad Prebys Aztec Student Union, San Diego State University, San Diego
CannonDesign

UCLA Medical Center, Santa Monica
Robert A.M. Stern Architects

Playhouse Plaza, Office and Retail, Pasadena
Moule & Polyzoides Architects and Urbanists

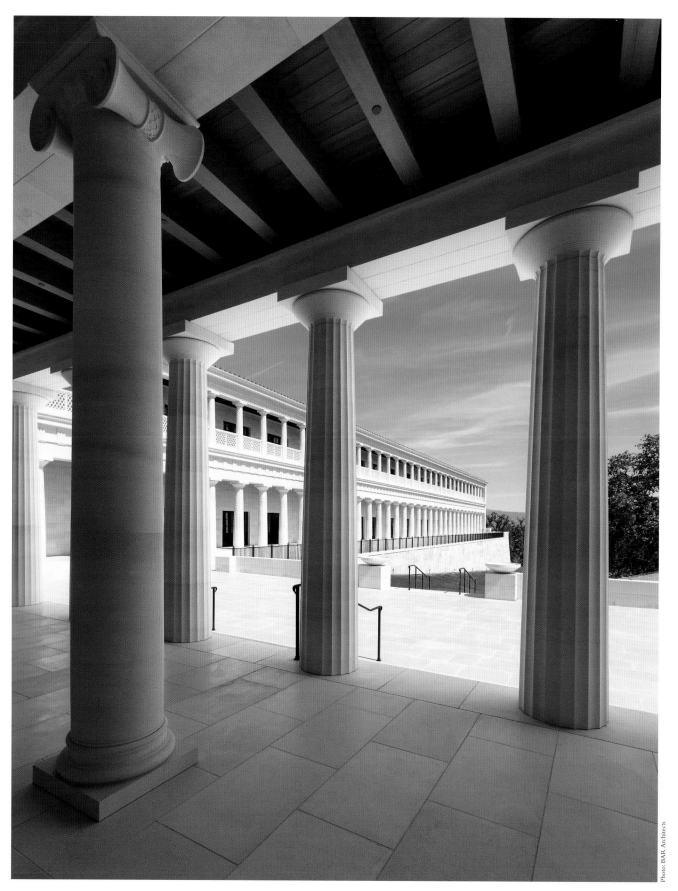

Photo: BAR Architects

The Packard Humanities Institute Film Archive and Preservation Center, Santa Clarita
BAR Architects   Landscape: SWA Group

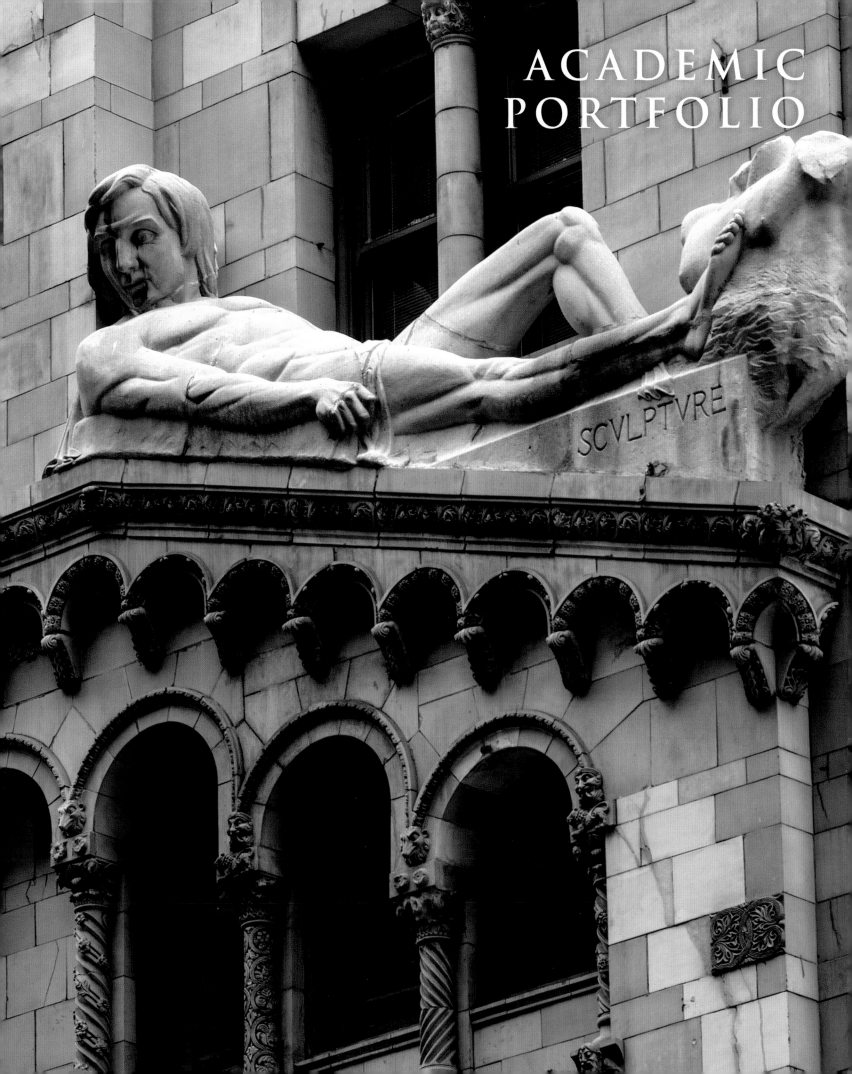

SCVLPTVRE

UNIVERSITY OF NOTRE DAME
Notre Dame, Indiana

Market and Railway Station, San Jacinto, California
Jeffrey Murillo, 5th Year, Instructors: Associate Professor Krupali Krusche and Dean Michael Lykoudis

Market Hall and Downtown Development, Lafayette, California
Alexander Preudhomme, 5th Year, Instructors: Associate Professor Krupali Krusche and Dean Michael Lykoudis

Symphony Hall, Chicago, Illinois
Xiaoyun Zhang, 1st Year Graduate, Instructor: Professor Duncan Stroik

Civic Club, Chicago, Illinois
Thomas P. Boyle, 5th Year, Instructor: Professor Duncan Stroik

Our Lady of the Oatka Abbey, Wheatland, New York
Matthew Hayes, 5th Year, Instructor: Professor Richard S. Bullene, C.S.C.

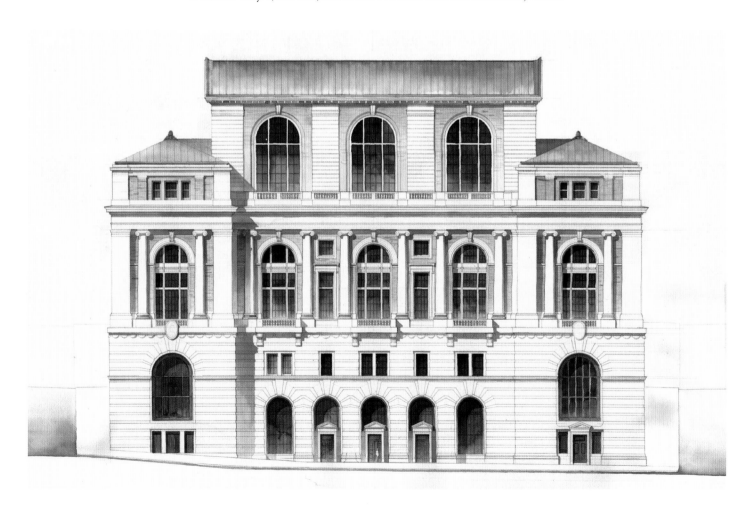

Counterproposal to the Seattle Public Library, Seattle, Washington
Parker Hanson, 5th Year, Instructor: Professor Duncan Stroik

UNIVERSITY OF NOTRE DAME
Notre Dame, Indiana

Single-family Residence, Palm Beach, Florida
Daniel Kiser, 2nd Year, Instructor: Adjunct Professor Jenny Bevan

Townhouse, Chicago, Illinois
Juan Salazar, 2nd Year,
Instructor: Adjunct Professor Jenny Bevan

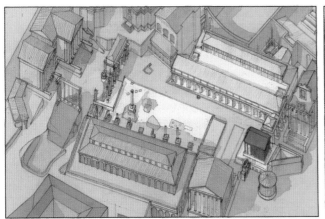

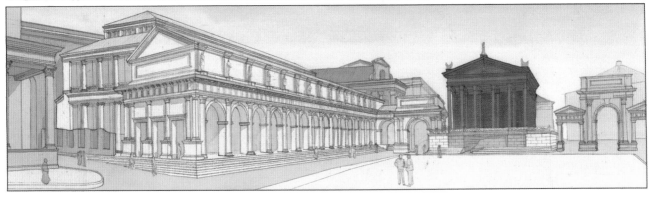

Conservation and Development Plan for the Roman Forum, Rome, Italy
Eric Stalheim, 2nd Year Graduate, M.S. in Historic Preservation, Instructor: Professor Stephen Semes

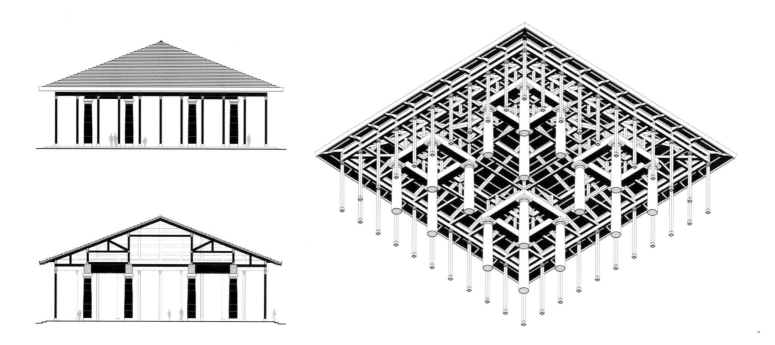

Market Building, Olympic Village, Rome, Italy
Dimitris Hartonas, 1st Year Graduate, Instructors: Elizabeth Moule and George Knight

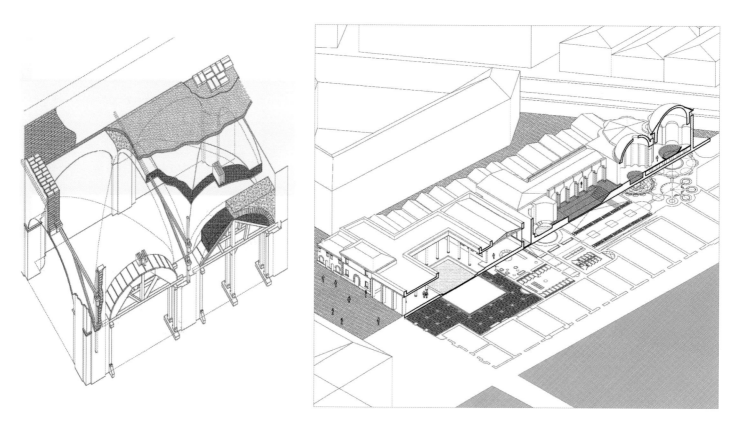

Baths, Olympic Village, Rome, Italy
Lucia Venditti, 1st Year Graduate, Instructors: Elizabeth Moule and George Knight

JUDSON UNIVERSITY
Elgin, Illinois

School for the Building Arts, Charleston, South Carolina
Lucas Stegeman, 4th Year, Instructor: Professor Christopher Miller

AUBURN UNIVERSITY
Auburn, Alabama

Analysis, San Carlo alle Quattro Fontane, Rome, Italy
Tina Malieri, 3rd Year, Instructor: Professor J. Scott Finn

Analysis, Palazzo Farnese, Rome, Italy
Peter McInish, 3rd Year, Instructor: Professor J. Scott Finn

INTBAU
Seville Traditional Architecture and Urbanism Summer School

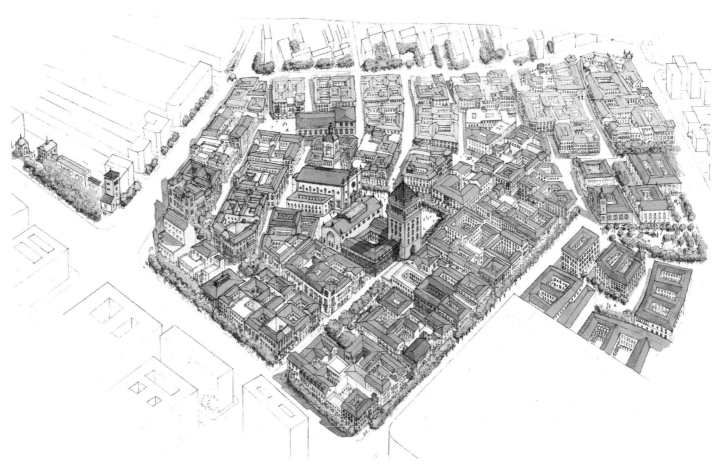

Counterproposal for Cruz del Campo, Seville, Spain
Instructors: Alejandro García Hermida, Frank Martínez, Lucien Steil, Samir Younés

INTBAU
Engelsberg Summer School in Classical Architecture

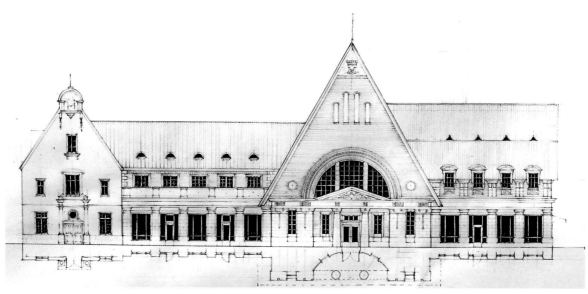

Galleria, Stora torget, Västerås, Sweden
Stephanie Jazmines, Instructors: Jenny Bevan and Christopher Liberatos

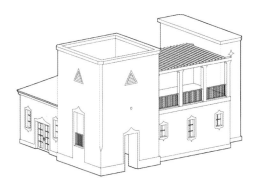

Communal Hall, Key West, Florida
Mackenzie Wilhelm, 1st Year, Instructor: Professor Victor Deupi

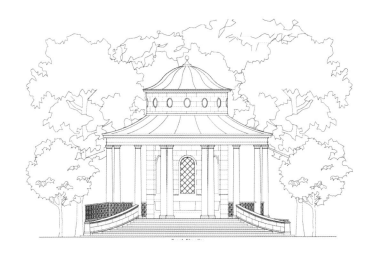
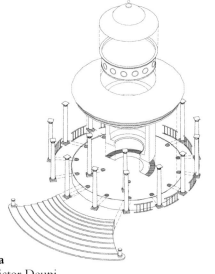

Coral Stone Corner, Key West, Florida
Cecelia McCammon, 1st Year, Instructor: Professor Victor Deupi

Tropical Park Fencing Academy, Miami, Florida
Maxwell Erickson, 2nd Year, Instructor: Professor Richard John

UNIVERSITY OF COLORADO
Denver, Colorado

Palladian House, Denver, Colorado
Kaitlyn Luzader, 3rd Year Graduate, Instructor: Professor Keith Loftin

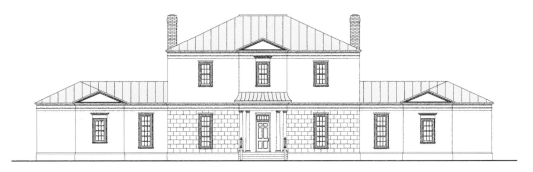

Palladian House, Denver, Colorado
Mason O'Farrell, 3rd Year Graduate, Instructor: Professor Keith Loftin

BENEDICTINE COLLEGE
Atchison, Kansas

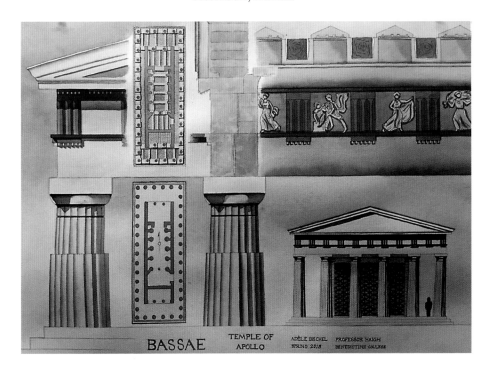

Analysis, Temple of Apollo, Bassae, Greece
Adele Bischel, 3rd Year, Instructor: Professor John Haigh

CATHOLIC UNIVERSITY OF AMERICA
Washington, D.C.

Museum of the United States Supreme Court, Washington, D.C.
Nicole A. Doyle, Timothy M. Farina, Daniel M. Glasgow, Mallory M. Smith, 4th Year, Instructor: James McCrery

KINGSTON UNIVERSITY
Kingston, England

Gallery for the Stour Valley, Sudbury, Suffolk, England
Clare Salter, 5th Year Postgraduate,
Instructors: Professors Timothy Smith and Jonathan Taylor

Office Building, The Strand, London, England
Line Young, 5th Year, Instructors: Professors Timothy Smith and
Jonathan Taylor

DUBLIN SCHOOL OF ARCHITECTURE
Dublin, Ireland

Measured Drawing, Russborough House, Blessington, Ireland
Conor Lynch, Independent Study

UNIVERSITY OF MARYLAND
College Park, Maryland

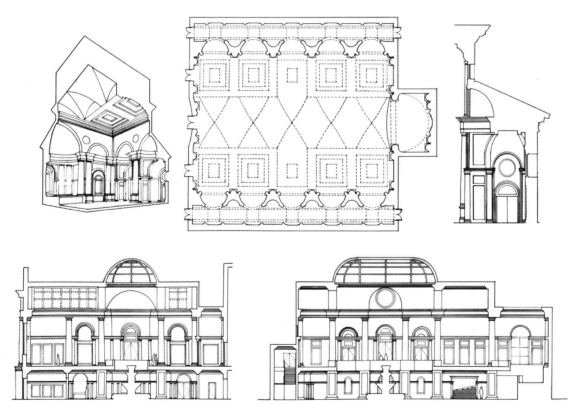

Promenade, Washington, D. C.
Trevor Wood, 2nd Year Graduate, Instructor: Professor Steven Hurtt

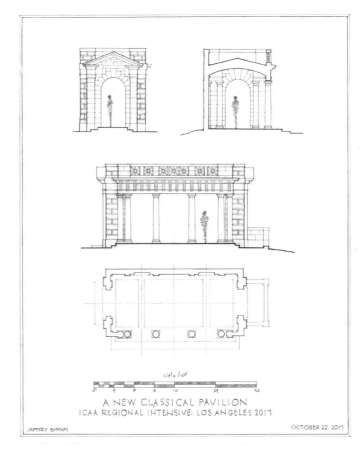

Continuing Education

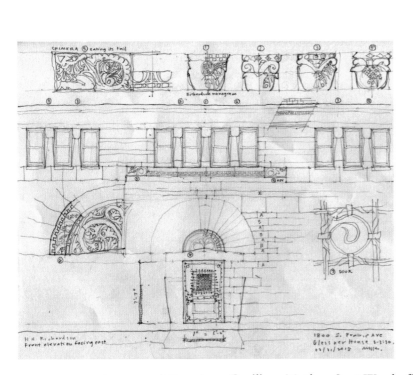

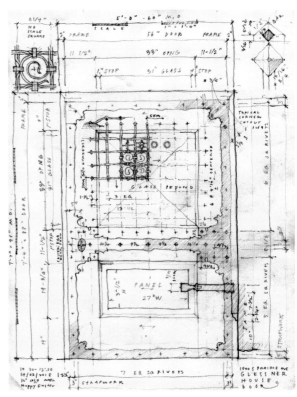

(UPPER LEFT) **Greystone Pavilion,** Matthew Scott Woodruff; (UPPER RIGHT) **Park Pavilion,** Jeffrey Bissiri,
Instructors: Chris Eiland, Erik Evens, Michael Mesko
(BOTTOM) **Chicago Chapter, Glessner House Measured Drawing**, Margaret Ketchum, Instructor: Stephen Chrisman

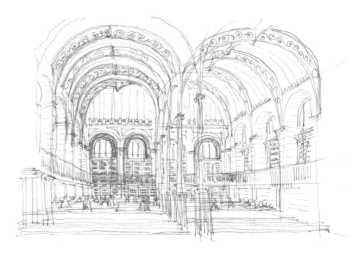

(UPPER LEFT) **Petit Trianon,** Cindy Black; (UPPER RIGHT) **Petit Trianon,** Elaine Rose;
(MIDDLE LEFT) **The French Pavilion and** (MIDDLE RIGHT) **Entrance to The Queens Theater, Domain du Petit Trianon,** Connor Moran;
(BOTTOM LEFT) **Place des Voges,** Ryan Hughes; (BOTTOM RIGHT) **Bibliothèque Sainte-Geneviève,** Elaine Rose,
Instructors: Kahlil Hamady, Leslie-Jon Vickory, Andrew Zega, Bernd Dams

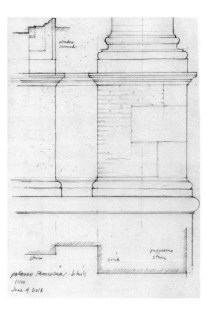

(UPPER LEFT) **Tempietto,** Jennifer Frantik; (UPPER RIGHT) **Villa Farnesina,** Cindy Black; (MIDDLE LEFT) **Arch of Septimius Severus,** Eric Kerke; (MIDDLE RIGHT) **Cancelleria,** Rick Swan; (BOTTOM) **Santa Maria Assunta,** Cindy Swan, Instructors: David Mayernik, Richard Piccolo, George Saumarez Smith, Brendan Hart

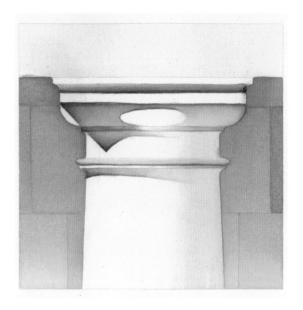

(UPPER LEFT) **Light and Shade Study,** Alessandra Giannasca, Colgate University, Instructor: Giuseppe Mazzone;
(UPPER RIGHT) **Ink Wash,** Kathryn Partin, Anderson Ariversity, Instructor: David Genther;
(BOTTOM) **Prospect Park Pavilion,** Timothy Farina, Catholic University of America,
Instructors: Keaton Bloom, Mark Santrach, Lora Shea, Michael Mesko, Javier Perez

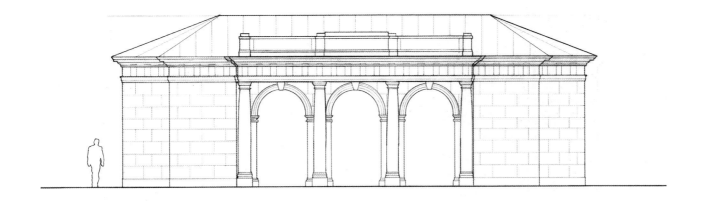

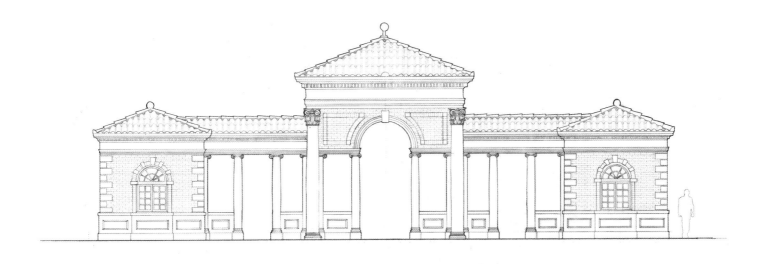

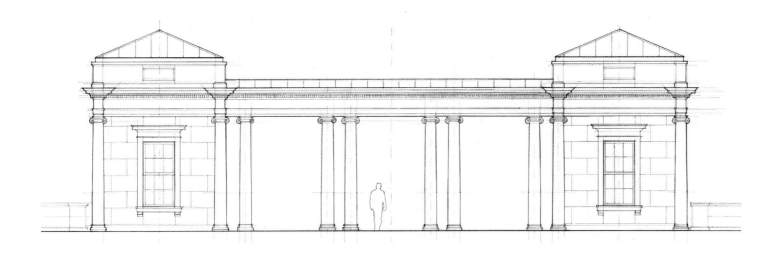

Prospect Park Pavilion: (UPPER) Margaret Jones, Benedictine College; (MIDDLE) Molly Kase, Alfred State College; (BOTTOM) Reed Thompson, Ball State University, Instructors: Keaton Bloom, Mark Santrach, Michael Mesko, Javier Perez

ACADEMY OF CLASSICAL DESIGN
Southern Pines, North Carolina

Ornament Study
Christian Nieto, Instructor: D. Jeffrey Mims

Ornament Study
Rodney Wilkinson, Instructor: D. Jeffrey Mims

GRAND CENTRAL ATELIER
Long Island City, New York

Study of Soldiers' and Sailors' Monument, New York, New York
Caeil Haigh, Instructor: Anthony Baus

TEN SIGNIFICANT CLASSICAL ARCHITECTURAL

DOWNTOWN LOS ANGELES

City Hall

Central Library

Union Station

Bradbury Building

Herald Examiner Building

PASADENA

City Hall

Central Library

Civic Auditorium

Caltech Athenaeum

The Huntington

LOS FELIZ AND HANCOCK PARK

Griffith Park

Griffith Observatory

Hancock Park Residences

United Methodist Church

El Royale

USC (University of Southern California) AND UCLA (University of California, Los Angeles)

Doheny Memorial Library, USC

Mudd Hall of Philosophy, USC

Clark Memorial Library, UCLA

Royce Hall, UCLA

Powell Library, UCLA

SANTA MONICA, VENICE, AND MALIBU

Santa Monica City Hall

Getty Villa Exterior

Getty Villa Interior

Adamson House

Windward Avenue Arcade

EXCURSIONS IN SOUTHERN CALIFORNIA

PALOS VERDES

Neptune Fountain,
Malaga Cove Plaza

Malaga Cove Plaza

Residences

Stables

Wayfarers Chapel

CLAREMONT AND POMONA

Tiernan Field House,
Scripps College

Browning Hall,
Scripps College

Fox Theater
Pomona

Pomona Station
Bridge

Pomona Station

RIVERSIDE

Mission Inn

Mission Inn Detail

County Courthouse

Art Museum

Universalist
Unitarian Church

SAN DIEGO

Rancho Santa Fe

Balboa Park
Lily Pond

Balboa Park
Botanical Building

Junipero Serra
Museum

La Jolla Woman's
Club

SANTA BARBARA

Old Mission

Arlington Theater

El Paseo
("Street in Spain")

Lobero Theatre

County Courthouse

SELECTED BIBLIOGRAPHY ON
SOUTHERN CALIFORNIA ARCHITECTURE

The following publications include examples from the beginning of the twentieth century, which witnessed a proliferation of drawing and photography books and folios depicting Mexican, Spanish, and Mediterranean architecture. These were produced by architects, photographers, and students making the grand tour of Europe and soon spawned more publications, including those featuring buildings that were contemporary Mediterranean and Spanish Colonial interpretations of the original precedents. The books were a valuable resource for local California architects and their clients, serving the same inspirational purpose then that current architectural "style" books do today.

Ames, Meriam. *Rancho Santa Fe: A California Village.* Rancho Santa Fe, CA: Rancho Santa Fe Society, 2001.

Appleton, Marc. *George Washington Smith: An Architect's Scrapbook.* Los Angeles: Tailwater Press, 2001.

Appleton, Marc, and Melba Levick. *California Mediterranean.* New York: Rizzoli International Publications, 2007.

Appleton, Marc, Bret Parsons, Steve Vaught. *Gordon B. Kaufmann: Master Architects of Southern California 1920–1940.* Los Angeles: Tailwater Press, 2016.

Aran, Berge, and Gail Jansen. *Austin Val Verde: A Montecito Masterpiece.* Santa Barbara, CA: Austin Val Verde Foundation, 2005.

Arte y Decoración en España. 10 vols. Barcelona: V. Casellas Moncanut, 1917.

Ayres, Atlee. *Mexican Architecture: Domestic, Civil and Ecclesiastical.* New York: William Helburn, 1926.

Banham, Reyner. *Los Angeles: The Architecture of Four Ecologies.* New York: Harper & Row, 1971, 1976.

Belloli, Jay, Charles Calvo, Alson Clark, Jan Furey Muntz, Stefanos Polyzoides. *Wallace Neff 1895–1982: The Romance of Regional Architecture.* San Marino, CA: The Huntington Library, 1989.

Bossom, Alfred C. *An Architectural Pilgrimage in Old Mexico.* New York: Charles Scribner's Sons, 1926.

Bottomley, William Lawrence. *Spanish Details.* New York: William Helburn, 1924.

Brasfield, John C., ed. *Architectural Digest: A Pictorial Digest of California's Best Architecture.* Los Angeles, esp. issues 1925–1940.

de Bretteville, Peter, and Stefanos Polyzoides, eds. *Caltech 1910–1950: An Urban Architecture for Southern California.* Pasadena, CA: Baxter Art Gallery, California Institute of Technology, 1983.

Bricker, Lauren Weiss, and Juergen Nogai. *The Mediterranean House in America.* New York: Harry N. Abrams, 2008.

Byne, Arthur, and Mildred Stapley Byne. *Decorated Wooden Ceilings in Spain.* New York: G. P. Putnam's Sons, 1920.

———. *Majorcan Houses and Gardens.* New York: William Helburn, 1928.

———. *Provincial Houses in Spain.* New York: William Helburn, 1927.

———. *Spanish Architecture of the Sixteenth Century.* New York: G. P. Putnam's Sons, 1917.

———. *Spanish Gardens and Patios: Philadelphia and London.* New York: J. B. Lippincott, 1924.

———. *Spanish Ironwork.* New York: Hispanic Society of America, 1915.

Chamberlain, Samuel. *Sketches of Northern Spanish Architecture.* New York: Architectural Book Publishing Co., 1926.

Chueca Goitia, Fernando, *Historia de la Arquitectura Española.* 2 vols. Madrid: Editorial Dossat, 1965.

Clark, Alson, Peter de Bretteville, Stefanos Polyzoides. *Myron Hunt 1868–1952: The Search for a Regional Architecture.* Santa Monica, CA: Hennessey and Ingalls, 1984.

Clark, Alson, Jan Furey Muntz, Jay Belloli, Stefanos Polyzoides. *Johnson, Kaufmann, Coate: Partners in the California Style.* Claremont, CA: Scripps College, 1992.

Clark, Alson, Wallace Neff Jr., David Gebhard. *Wallace Neff: Architect of California's Golden Age.* Santa Barbara, CA: Capra Press, 1986.

Clark, Robert Judson, and Thomas S. Hines. *Los Angeles Transfer: Architecture in Southern California 1880–1980.* Los Angeles: William Andrews Clark Memorial Library, University of California, Los Angeles, 1983.

Clute, Eugene. *Masterpieces of Spanish Architecture: Romanesque and Allied Styles.* New York: Pencil Points Press, 1925.

Collantes de Terán y Delorme, Francisco, and Luis Gómez Estern. *Arquitectura Civil Sevillana.* Seville: Ayuntamiento, 1976.

Cram, Ralph Adams. *American Country Houses of Today.* New York: Architectural Book Publishing Co., 1913.

Deverell, William. *Whitewashed Adobe.* Berkeley, CA: University of California Press, 2004.

Diaz Recasens, Gonzalo. *Plazas de Toros*. Seville: Consejería de Obras Públicas y Transportes, 1992.

Dobyns, Winifred Starr, and Myron Hunt. *California Gardens*. New York: Macmillan Co., 1931.

Eberlein, H. D. *Villas of Florence and Tuscany*. Philadelphia: J. B. Lippincott, 1922.

Feduchi, Luis. *Itinerarios de Arquitectura Popular Española*. 5 vols. Barcelona: Editorial Blume, 1974–84.

Fink, Augusta. *Palos Verdes Peninsula*. Lafayette, CA: Great West Books, 2004.

————. *Time and the Terraced Land*, Berkeley, CA: Howell-North Books, 1966.

Flores, Carlos. *Arquitectura Popular Española*. 5 vols. Madrid: Editorial Aguilar, 1973–77.

Forestier, J.C.N. *Gardens: A Note-Book of Plans and Sketches*. New York: Charles Scribner's Sons, 1928.

Fox, Helen Morgenthau. *Patio Gardens*. New York: Macmillan Co., 1929.

Garnett, Porter, and Bruce Porter. *Stately Homes of California*. Boston: Little, Brown & Co., 1915.

Garrison, Richard, and George Rustay. *Mexican Houses*. New York; Architectural Book Publishing Co., 1930.

Gebhard, David. *George Washington Smith 1876–1930: The Spanish Colonial Revival in California*. Exh. cat. Santa Barbara, CA: The Art Gallery, University of California, Santa Barbara, 1964.

————. *Santa Barbara—The Creation of a New Spain in America*. Exh. cat. Santa Barbara, CA: University Art Museum, 1982.

————. "The Spanish Colonial Revival in Southern California (1895–1930)." *Journal of the Society of Architectural Historians* 26, no. 2 (May 1967): 131–47.

Gebhard, David, and Harriette Von Breton. *Architecture in California 1868–1968*. Exh. cat. Santa Barbara, CA:

The Art Galleries, University of California Santa Barbara, 1968.

Gebhard, David, and Sheila Lynds, eds. *An Arcadian Landscape: The California Gardens of A. E. Hanson*. Los Angeles: Hennessey & Ingalls, 1985.

Gebhard, David, and Robert Winter. *A Guide to Architecture in Los Angeles & Southern California*. Salt Lake City: Peregrine Smith, 1977.

Gebhard Patricia. *George Washington Smith: Architect of the Spanish Colonial Revival*. Salt Lake City: Gibbs, Smith, 2005.

Gladding, McBean and Co. *Latin Tiles*. San Francisco: Taylor & Taylor, 1923.

Goodhue, Bertram G. *The Architecture and the Gardens of the San Diego Exposition*. San Francisco: Paul Elder & Co., 1916.

————. *A Book of Architectural and Decorative Drawings*. New York: Architectural Book Publishing Co., 1914.

Hales, Michael, Nancy Goslee Power, Susan Heeger. *The Gardens of California*. Santa Monica, CA: Hennessey & Ingalls, 2001.

Hannaford, Donald R., and Revel Edwards. *Spanish Colonial or Adobe Architecture of California 1800–1850*. New York: Architectural Book Publishing Co., 1931.

Hielscher, Kurt. *Picturesque Spain*. New York: Brentano's, 1928.

Hooker, Marian Osgood. *Farmhouses and Small Provincial Buildings in Southern Italy*. New York: Architectural Book Publishing Co., 1925.

Hunter, Paul Robinson, and Walter E. Reichardt. *Residential Architecture in Southern California, 1939*. Santa Monica, CA: Hennessey & Ingalls, 1998.

Kanner, Diane. *Wallace Neff and the Grand Houses of the Golden State*. New York: The Monacelli Press, 2005.

Kaplan, Sam Hall. *L. A. Lost and Found*. Los Angeles: Angel City Press, 2002.

Kirker, Harold. *California's Architectural Frontier: Style and Tradition in the Nineteenth Century*. San Marino, CA: The Huntington Library, 1960.

————. *Old Forms on a New Land: California Architecture in Perspective*. Niwot, CO: Roberts Rinehart Publications, 1991.

La Beaume, Louis, and William Booth Papin. *The Picturesque Architecture of Mexico*. New York: Architectural Book Publishing Co., 1915.

Lowell, Guy. *Smaller Italian Villas and Farmhouses*. 2 vols. New York: Architectural Book Publishing Co., 1920, 1922.

Mack, Gerstle, and Thomas Gibson. *Architectural Details of Northern and Central Spain*. New York: William Helburn, 1928.

————. *Architectural Details of Southern Spain*. New York: William Helburn, 1928.

Masson, Kathryn. *Santa Barbara Style*. New York: Rizzoli International Publications, 2001.

Masson, Kathryn, Lauren Weiss Bricker, Paul Rocheleau, Robert Winter. *The California House*. New York: Rizzoli International Publications, 2011.

Mayer, August L. *Old Spain*. New York: Brentano's, 1921.

McCall, Wayne, Herb Andree, Noel Young, Patricia Halloran. *Santa Barbara Architecture*. Santa Barbara, CA: Capra Press, 1975.

McChung, William Alexander. *Landscapes of Desire: Anglo Mythologies of Los Angeles*. Berkeley, CA: University of California Press, 2002.

McMillian, Elizabeth. *California Colonial: The Spanish and Rancho Revival Styles*. Atglen, PA: Schiffer Publishing, 2002.

————. *Casa California: Spanish-Style Houses from Santa Barbara to San Clemente*. Rizzoli International Publications, 1996.

Michael, A. C. *An Artist in Spain*. London: Hodder & Stoughton, 1920.

Moore, Charles, Peter Becker, Regula Campbell. *The City Observed: Los Angeles*. New York: Vintage Books, 1984.

Mundigo, Axel I., Daniel J. Garr, Dora P. Crouch. *Spanish City Planning in North America.* Cambridge, MA: MIT Press, 1982.

Myrick, David F. *Montecito and Santa Barbara.* 2 vols. Pasadena, CA: Pentrex Media Group, 1988.

Neff, Wallace. *Architecture of Southern California.* Chicago: Rand McNally & Co., 1966.

Newcomb, Rexford. *Franciscan Mission Architecture of California.* Mineola, NY: Dover Publications, 1989.

————. *Mediterranean Domestic Architecture in the United States.* Cleveland: J. H. Jansen, 1928. Repr. by Acanthus Press, 1999.

————. *The Old Mission Churches and Historical Houses of California.* J. B. Lippincott, 1925.

————. *Spanish-Colonial Architecture in the United States.* New York: J. J. Augustin, 1937.

————. *The Spanish House for America, Its Design, Furnishing, and Garden.* Philadelphia: J. B. Lippincott, 1927.

Nichols, Rose Standish. *Spanish & Portuguese Gardens.* New York: Houghton Mifflin, 1924.

Nierman, Daniel, and Ernesto Vallejo. *The Hacienda in Mexico.* Translated by Mardith Schuetz-Miller. Austin: University of Texas Press, 2003.

Oliver, Richard. *Bertram Grosvenor Goodhue.* New York: The Architectural History Foundation, 1983.

Padilla, Victoria. *Southern California Gardens: An Illustrated History.* Berkeley, CA: University of California Press, 1961.

Polyzoides, Stefanos, Roger Sherwood, James Tice. *Courtyard Housing in Los Angeles.* Berkeley, CA: University of California Press, 1982.

Prentice, Andrew N. *Renaissance Architecture and Ornament in Spain.* New York: Paul Wenzel, n.d.

Prieto Moreno, Francisco. *Los Jardines de Granada.* Madrid: Dirección

General de Bellas Artes, Ministerio de Educación y Ciencia, Patronato Nacional de Museos, 1973.

Requa, Richard. *Architectural Details: Spain and the Mediterranean.* Los Angeles: Monolith Portland Cement Co., 1926.

————. *Inside Lights on the Building of San Diego's Exposition 1935.* San Diego, CA: Parker H. Jackson, 1997.

————. *Old World Inspiration for American Architecture.* Los Angeles: Monolith Portland Cement Co., 1929.

Sexton, Randolph W. *Spanish Influence on American Architecture and Decoration.* New York: Brantano's, 1927.

Soule, Winsor. *Spanish Farm Houses and Minor Public Buildings.* New York: Architectural Book Publishing Co., 1924.

Staats, H. Philip. *Californian Architecture in Santa Barbara.* New York: Architectural Book Publishing Co., 1929. Repr. 1990.

Stanton, J. E. *By Middle Seas: Photographic Studies Reflecting the Architectural Motives of Various Cities on the Mediterranean.* Los Angeles: Gladding, McBean and Co., 1927.

Starr, Kevin. *Inventing the Dream: California through the Progressive Era.* New York: Oxford University Press, 1985.

————. *Material Dreams: Southern California through the 1920s.* New York: Oxford University Press, 1991.

Streatfield, David C. *California Gardens: Creating a New Eden.* New York: Abbeville Press, 1994.

Sweeney, Robert. *Casa del Herrero.* New York: Rizzoli International Publications, 2009.

Tilman, Jeffrey T. *Arthur Brown Jr.: Progressive Classicist.* New York: W. W. Norton, 2006.

Van Pelt, Garrett. *Old Architecture of Southern Mexico.* Cleveland: J. H. Jansen, 1926.

Villa Narcissa: An Italian Garden in California. N.p.: Friends of French Art, 1992.

Waldie, D. J., and Douglas Woods. *Classic Homes of Los Angeles.* New York: Rizzoli International Publications, 2010.

Watters, Sam. *Houses of Los Angeles, 1895–1919.* New York: Acanthus Press, 2007.

————. *Houses of Los Angeles, 1920–1935.* New York: Acanthus Press, 2007.

Weitze, Karen J. *California's Mission Revival.* Santa Monica, CA: Hennessey & Ingalls, 1984.

Welch, Diane Y. *Lilian J. Rice: Architect of Rancho Santa Fe, California.* Atglen, PA: Schiffer Publishing, 2010.

Whitaker, Charles H. *Bertram Grosvenor Goodhue, Architect and Master of Many Arts.* New York: Press of the American Institute of Architects, 1925. Repr. by Da Capo Press, 1976.

Whittlesey, Austin. *The Minor Ecclesiastical, Domestic, and Garden Architecture of Southern Spain.* New York: Architectural Book Publishing Co., 1917.

————. *The Renaissance Architecture of Central and Northern Spain.* New York: Architectural Book Publishing Co., 1920.

Woodbridge, Sally Byrne, Stanley Young, Melba Levick. *The Missions of California.* San Francisco: Chronicle Books, 2004.

Woods, Douglas. *Classic Homes of Los Angeles.* New York: Rizzoli International Publications, 2010.

Wyllie, Romy. *Caltech's Architectural Heritage: From Spanish Tile to Modern Stone.* Los Angeles: Balcony Press, 2000.

Yerbury, F. B. *Lesser Known Architecture of Spain.* New York: William Helburn, 1926.

Zarakov, Barry Neil. "California Planned Communities of the 1920s." Master's thesis. University of California, Santa Barbara, 1977.

ONG-ARD ARCHITECTS
Architecture & Planning

Chiang Mai, Thailand | ongardarchitects.com

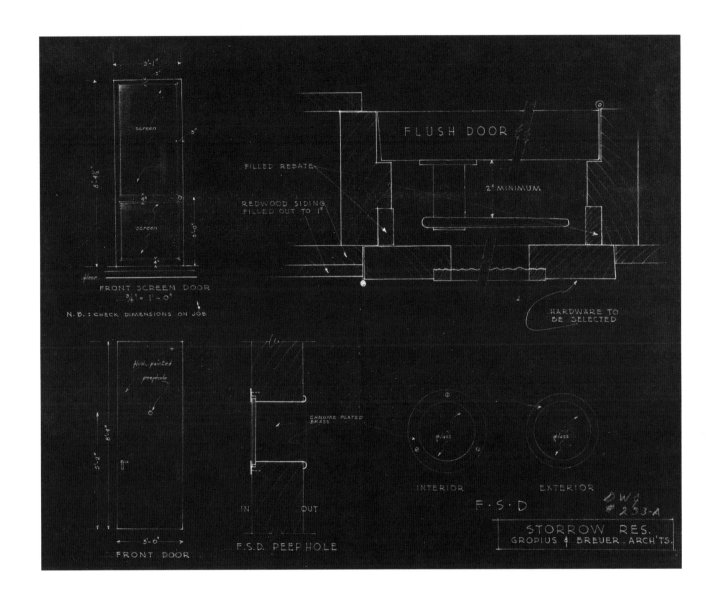

"STORROW RES.," GROPIUS & BREUER ARCHITECTS BLUEPRINT

W.C. Vaughan Co. Archives, Drawing No. 233-A, 1938

E.R. Butler & Co. Research Library

ROCKEFELLER APARTMENTS

Wallace Kirkman Harrison, Architect

NEW YORK, NY

1936

NATHANIEL SALTONSTALL HOUSE

Saltonstall & Morton, Architects

MEDFIELD, MA

1937

CHRIST CHURCH CRANBROOK

Bertram Grosvenor Goodhue, Architect

1938

WILLIAM P. BARTEL HOUSE

Eleanor Raymond, Architect

WAYLAND, MA

1938

PILLSBURY SUMMER HOUSE

Eleanor Raymond & Sarah Pillsbury Harkness, Architects

DUXBURY, MA

1938

EXMOOR FARM RENOVATION

Eleanor Raymond, Architect

WESTON, MA

Ca. 1938

GROPIUS HOUSE

Walter Gropius & Marcel Breuer, Architects

LINCOLN, MA

1938

MR. & MRS. G. HOLMES PERKINS HOUSE

George Holmes Perkins, Architect

BROOKLINE, MA

1938–1939

JOSEPHINE M. HAGERTY HOUSE

Walter Gropius & Marcel Breuer, Architects

COHASSET, MA

1938–1939

BREUER HOUSE, LINCOLN

Marcel Breuer, Architect

LINCOLN, MA

1938–1939

UNKNOWN RETAIL STORE*

Eleanor Le Maire, Architect

1938

ARGENTINIAN PAVILION

Armando D'ans & Aymar Embury II, Architects

NEW YORK WORLD'S FAIR

NEW YORK, NY

1939

FORD HOUSE

Walter Gropius & Marcel Breuer, Architects

LINCOLN, MA

1939

FISCHER HOUSE & STUDIO
"WALDENMARK"

Walter Gropius & Marcel Breuer, Architects

WRIGHTSTOWN TOWNSHIP, BUCKS COUNTY, PA

1939

LIFE MAGAZINE'S LIFE HOUSES
"TOWN OF TOMORROW"

NEW YORK WORLD'S FAIR

QUEENS, NY

1939, 1940

PENNSYLVANIA STATE EXHIBITION

NEW YORK WORLD'S FAIR

NEW YORK, NY

1939

TERZAGHI HOUSE

George Holmes Perkins, Architect

WINCHESTER, MA

1939–1940

GRIFFEN HOUSE

Fordyce & Hamby and George Nelson, Architects

SCARSDALE, NY

1939

ALAN I W FRANK HOUSE

Walter Gropius & Marcel Breuer, Architects

PITTSBURGH, PA

1940

Source: E.R. Butler & Co Research Library: W.C. Vaughan Co. Archives.

* *Archival Record Incomplete.*

PEABODY PLYWOOD HOUSE

Eleanor Raymond, Architect

DOVER, MA

1940

PLASTICS, 1940

Robert Woods Kennedy, Curator

INSTITUTE OF MODERN ART

BOSTON, MA

1940

9 ASH STREET HOUSE
"THESIS HOUSE"

Philip Cortelyou Johnson, Architect

CAMBRIDGE, MA

1941–1942

JOHN P. MONKS HOUSE

George Holmes Perkins, Architect

LINCOLN, MA

1941

CHAMBERLAIN COTTAGE

Marcel Breuer, Architect

WAYLAND, MA

1941

WEIZENBLATT HOUSE

Marcel Breuer, Architect

ASHEVILLE, NC

1941

ABELE HOUSE

Walter Gropius & Marcel Breuer, Architects

FRAMINGHAM, MA

1941

JACKSON HOUSE

Elliot Noyes, Architect
George Holmes Perkins, Supervising Architect

DOVER, MA

1941

NELSON ROCKEFELLER APARTMENT
810 FIFTH AVENUE

Wallace Kirkman Harrison, Architect
Jean-Michel Frank, Interior Design

NEW YORK, NY

1941

FARNSWORTH HOUSE

Ludwig Mies van der Rohe, Architect

PLANO, IL

1945–1951

GELLER HOUSE I

Marcel Breuer, Architect

LAWRENCE, NY

1945–1946

GILBERT TOMPKINS HOUSE

Marcel Breuer, Architect

HEWLETT HARBOR, NY

1946

THE GLASS HOUSE

Philip Cortelyou Johnson, Architect

NEW CANAAN, CT

1947–1949

BREUER COTTAGE

Marcel Breuer, Architect

WELLFLEET, MA

1948–1949

BREUER HOUSE I

Marcel Breuer, Architect

NEW CANAAN, CT

1948

EDWARD E. MILLS HOUSE

Marcel Breuer (Addition), 1951
Marcel Breuer (Alteration), 1954

NEW CANAAN, CT

1948

FISCHER GUEST COTTAGE

Marcel Breuer, Architect

NEWTOWN, PA

1948

KEPES COTTAGE

Marcel Breuer, Architect

WELLFLEET, MA

1948–1949

ROBINSON HOUSE

Marcel Breuer, Architect

WILLIAMSTOWN, MA

1948

E. R. Butler & Co.

Selected Modern Projects

Enoch Robinson & Henry Whitney (1826)

E. & G.W. Robinson & Co. (1837–1839)

E. Robinson & Co. (1839–1905)

Wm. Hall & Co. (1843–1921)

G.N. Wood & Co. (1905–1914)

John Tein Company (1883–1939)

L.S. Hall & Co. (1914–1918)

W.C. Vaughan Co. (1895-2000)

Ostrander & Eshleman (1921–1992)

Quincy Spindle Mfg. Co. (–1999)

(New England Lock and Hardware Co.)

Edward R. Butler Company (1966–1990)

&

E.R. Butler & Co. (1990–)

WALTER GROPIUS HOUSE, LINCOLN, MA

Ise Gropius Relaxing on Second Floor Terrace

Photographed by Robert Damora, 1948

BRANDEIS UNIVERSITY CHAPELS

Harrison & Abramovitz, Architects

Eero Saarinen, Master Plan

WALTHAM, MA

1954–1963

CHERMAYEFF COTTAGE & STUDIO*

Serge Chermayeff, Architect

WELLFLEET, MA

1954, 1958

BOWDITCH HOUSE

Eleanor Raymond, Architect

CAMBRIDGE, MA

1955

MOSLEY HOUSE*

The Architects Collaborative (TAC), Alteration

1955

MONSANTO HOUSE OF THE FUTURE

Richard Hamilton & Marvin Goody (MIT), Architects

TOMORROWLAND

DISNEYLAND, ANAHEIM, CA

1957

HOOPER HOUSE II

Herbert Beckhard & Marcel Breuer, Architects

BALTIMORE, MD

1958–1959

MURCHISON HOUSE

The Architects Collaborative (TAC), Architects

PROVINCETOWN, MA

1959

SAMUEL & MINETTE KUHN HOUSE

Saltonstall & Morton, Architects

WELLFLEET, MA

1960

ROYAL DANISH EMBASSY

Vilhelm Lauritzen Arkitekter, Architects

The Architects Collaborative (TAC), Consulting Architect

WASHINGTON, DC

1960

EMBASSY OF THE UNITED STATES

Walter Gropius, Pietro Belluschi & The Architects Collaborative (TAC), Architects

ATHENS, GREECE

1961

SOCIAL SCIENCE BUILDING

The Architects Collaborative (TAC), Architects

BRANDEIS UNIVERSITY

WALTHAM, MA

1961

BOSTON SAFE DEPOSIT & TRUST COMPANY

The Architects Collaborative (TAC), Architects

BOSTON, MA

1961

PHILLIPS ACADEMY

The Architects Collaborative (TAC), Architects

ANDOVER, MA

1961

JOSEPH M. EDINBURG HOUSE

Saltonstall & Morton, Architects

BROOKLINE, MA

1962

NEW ENGLAND STATES EXHIBITION

Campbell & Aldrich, Architects

NEW YORK WORLD'S FAIR

NEW YORK, NY

1962

CHERMAYEFF COURTYARD HOUSE

Serge Chermayeff, Architect

NEW HAVEN, CT

1962

EARTH SCIENCE BUILDING

Araldo Cossutta & I.M. Pei, Architects

THE MASSACHUSETTS INSTITUTE OF TECHNOLOGY (MIT)

CAMBRIDGE, MA

1962

CLARK ART INSTITUTE

Pietro Belluschi, Architect

WILLIAMSTOWN, MA

1972

KNIFFIN HOUSE

Marcel Breuer & Elliot Noyes, Architects

NEW CANAAN, CT

1949

SCOTT HOUSE

Marcel Breuer, Architect

DENNIS, MA

1949

HOUSE IN THE MUSEUM GARDEN

Marcel Breuer, Architect

MUSEUM OF MODERN ART (MoMA)

POCANTICO HILLS, NY

1949–1950

THOMPSON HOUSE
"WONDERWOOD"

Marcel Breuer, Architect

LIGONIER, PA

1949

SIX MOON HILL

The Architects Collaborative (TAC), Architects

LEXINGTON, MA

1949–1950

MAYO HILL COLONY CLUB

Saltonstall & Morton, Architects

WELLFLEET, MA

1949

WELLESLEY VETERANS HOUSING

Hugh Asher Stubbins, Architect

WELLESLEY, MA

1949–1952

SMITH HOUSE

Marcel Breuer, Architect

ASPEN, CO

1950

LAUCK HOUSE

Marcel Breuer, Architect

PRINCETON, NJ

1950

ZIMMERMAN HOUSE

Frank Lloyd Wright, Architect

MANCHESTER, NH

1950

HOWLETT HOUSE

The Architects Collaborative (TAC), Architects

BELMONT, MA

1950

MENIL HOUSE

Philip Cortelyou Johnson, Architect

HOUSTON, TX

1950–1951

PACK HOUSE

Marcel Breuer, Architect

SCARSDALE, NY

1951

WOLFSON TRAILER HOUSE

Marcel Breuer, Architect

SALT POINT, NY

1951

FIVE FIELDS

The Architects Collaborative (TAC), Architects

LEXINGTON, MA

1951–1957

P.M. HERZOG HOUSE

Huson Jackson, Architect

BOSTON, MA

1953

SCOTT RESIDENCE

Serge Chermayeff, Architect

WELLFLEET, MA

1954

GAGARIN HOUSE

Herbert Beckhard & Marcel Breuer, Architects

LITCHFIELD, CT

1954–1956

FIRST LUTHERAN CHURCH

Pietro Belluschi, Architect

BOSTON, MA

1954–1957

FALL 2018

"TRANSITIONAL MOMENTS:

MARCEL BREUER, THE W.C. VAUGHAN CO.,

& THE BAUHAUS IN AMERICA"

Robert Wiesenberger

Catalogue Entries by H. Reynolds Butler

"MANUFACTURING MODERNISM:

WALTER GROPIUS, MARCEL BREUER,

& THE W.C. VAUGHAN CO."

H. Reynolds Butler

Foreword by Peter McMahon

CATALOGUES AVAILABLE TO THE TRADE

WWW.ERBUTLER.COM

Drawings: Elmer Hale Pratt · Typography: John Packer · Photograph: Robert Damora © Damora Archive

G. P. Schafer Architect

— ARCHITECTURE & DESIGN —

GPSCHAFER.COM

RICHARD MANION

ARCHITECTURE INC.

DUNCAN MCROBERTS

A S S O C I A T E S

CLASSICAL ARCHITECTURE
...bespoke design from vernacular to high style...

A New Preparatory School

ERIC J. SMITH ARCHITECT

Photo Courtesy of Nathan Kirkman

THOMAS PROCTOR ARCHITECT

LOS ANGELES, CALIFORNIA
THOMASPROCTORARCHITECT.COM
310.913.0911

MARK P. FINLAY ARCHITECTS, AIA

ARCHITECTURE & INTERIOR DESIGN

L. LUMPKINS ARCHITECTS, INC.

214.730.0112   WWW.LUMPKINSARCHITECTS.COM

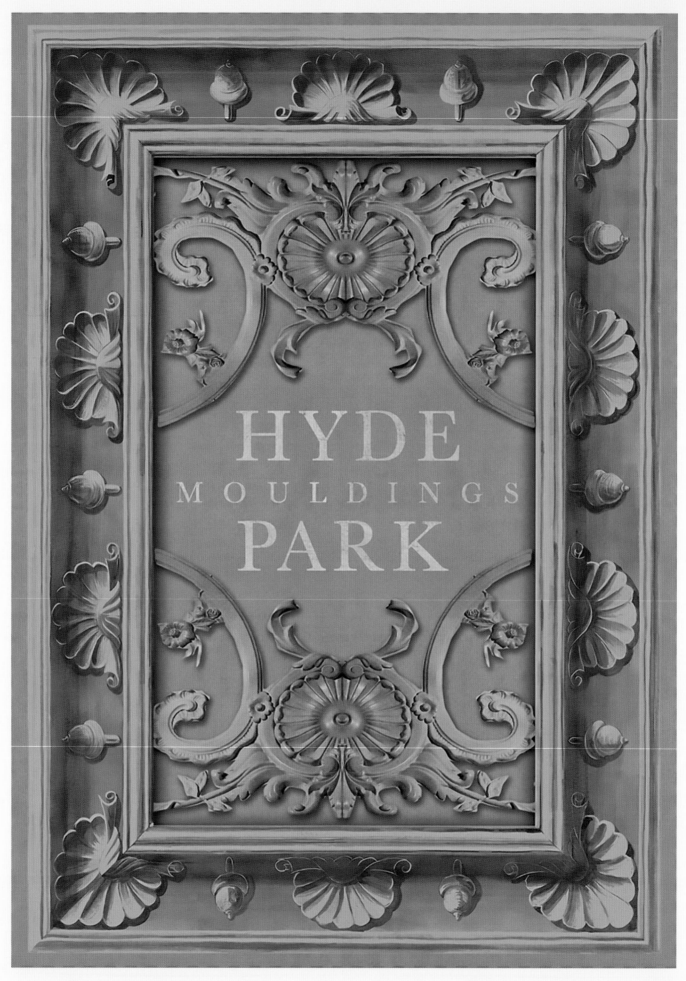

HYDE

MOULDINGS

PARK

North America's premier stewards of traditional plastercraft
www.hyde-park.com   631.PLASTER

HISTORICAL CONCEPTS

ARCHITECTURE & PLANNING

ATLANTA ~ NEW YORK

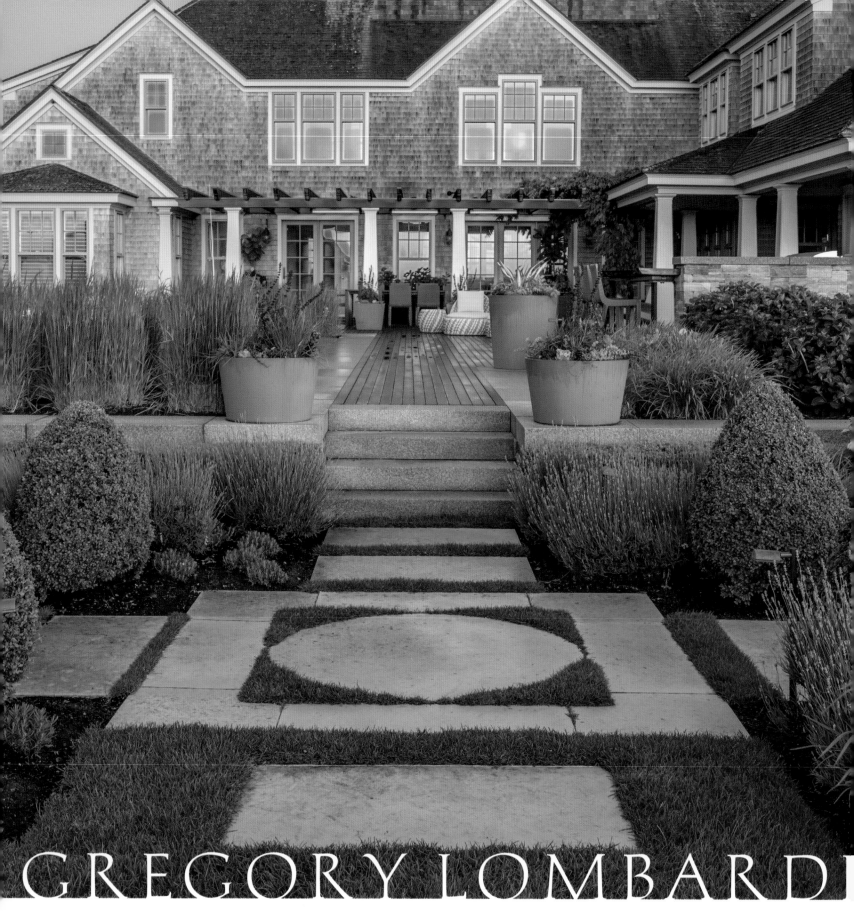

GREGORY LOMBARDI

Landscape Architecture

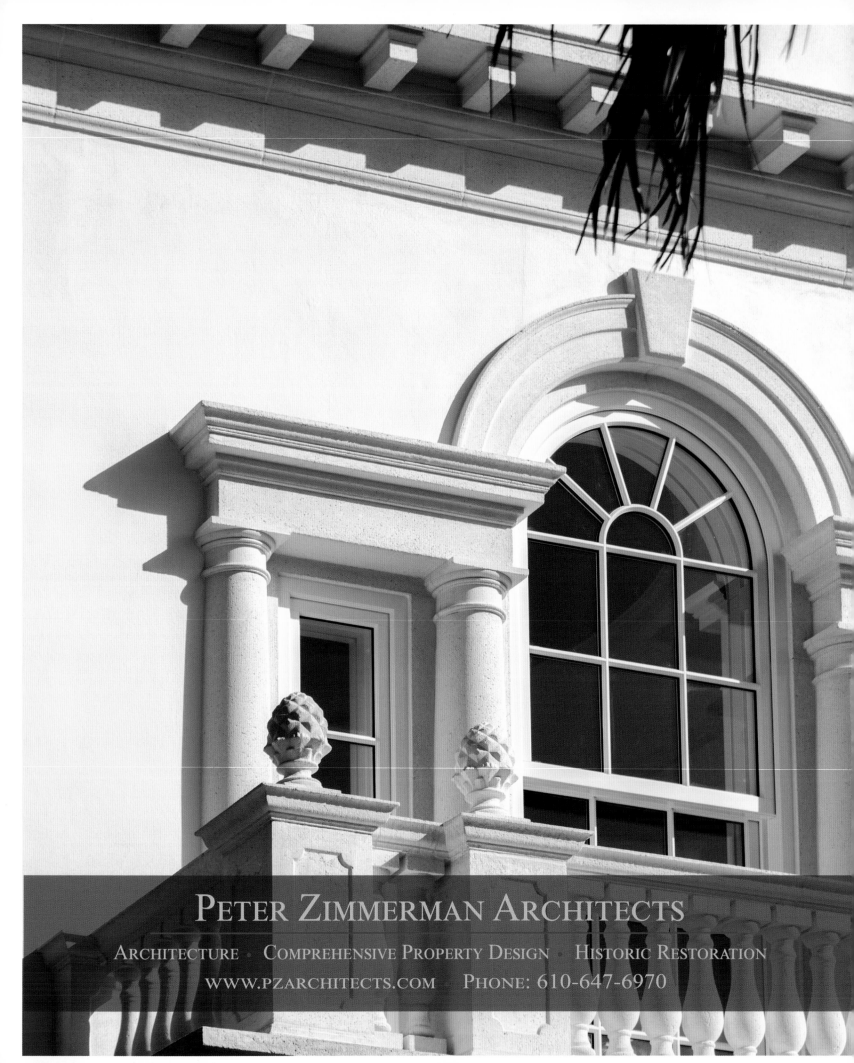

HARRISON
DESIGN

ARCHITECTURE
INTERIOR DESIGN - LANDSCAPE ARCHITECTURE

ANDREW V. GIAMBERTONE
& ASSOCIATES, ARCHITECTS

62 Elm St. * Huntington, NY * 631-367-0050 * GiambertoneArchitects.com

Chadsworth Incorporated

www.COLUMNS.com

1-800-COLUMNS
T +800 486 2118   F +910 763 3191

Architecture by Robert A.M. Stern Architects;
Gary Brewer, Partner; ramsa.com
Interior Design by S.R. Gambrel Inc.
Photography © Peter Aaron/Otto

DANGORDON
LANDSCAPEARCHITECTS

WELLESLEY ~ EDGARTOWN
DANGORDON.COM

2 IRONWORK & GLASS TRIM PROFILE
A-409 SCALE: FULL

3 CENTRAL BAND PROFILE
A-409 SCALE: FULL

4 THRESHOLD DETAIL
A-409 SCALE: FULL

1 ENTRY DOOR 100 DETAILS
A-409 SCALE : 3" = 1' 0"

5 ASTRAGAL DETAIL
A-409 SCALE: FULL

ENTRY DOOR DETALS

OLIVER COPE · ARCHITECT

135 WEST TWENTY-SIXTH STREET, NEW YORK, NEW YORK 10001

www.olivercope.com   (212) 727-1225

Jamb.

Mantels | Lighting | Furniture

+44 20 7730 2122 | jamb.co.uk

JOHN B. MURRAY ARCHITECT

48 WEST 37th STREET, 10th FLOOR, NEW YORK, NY 10018
JBMARCHITECT.COM
212-242-8600

FERGUS GARBER YOUNG ARCHITECTS

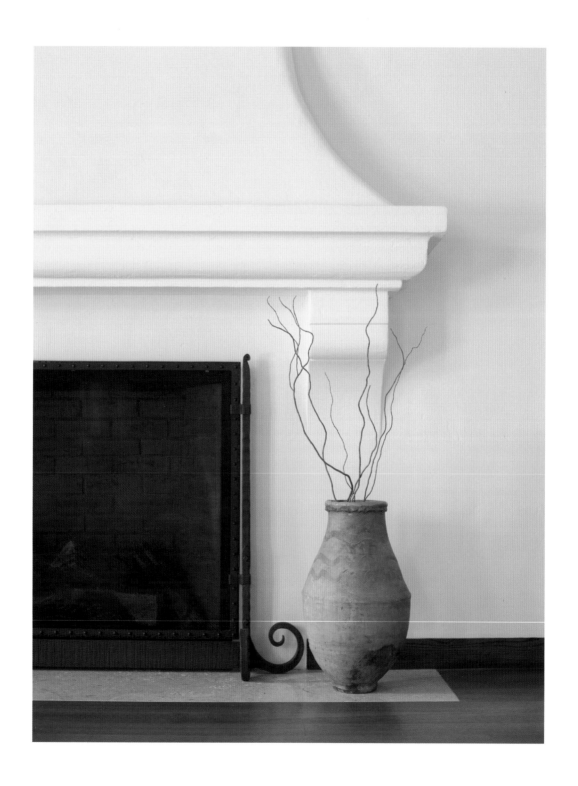

Suzanne Rheinstein & Associates

suzannerheinstein.com | Photo by Pieter Estersohn

PETER PENNOYER ARCHITECTS
PPAPC.COM

— A House in Coastal Maine —

T&M

TUCKER & MARKS INC

DESIGN

t: 415.445.6789   www.tuckerandmarks.com

HORIZON

BUILDERS

HorizonBuildersInc.net | 800-726-4876

Le George
at Four Seasons Hotel George V, Paris

PIERRE-YVES ROCHON

PARIS | CHICAGO

THE WRIGLEY BUILDING

410 NORTH MICHIGAN AVENUE, SUITE 1600, CHICAGO, ILLINOIS 60611

TEL +1 312 980 7700 FAX +1 312 980 7710

INFO@PYR-DESIGN.COM, WWW.PYR-DESIGN.COM

VELLA INTERIORS

BUILDERS OF EXQUISITE RESIDENCES

118 Bay Avenue, Huntington Bay, N.Y. 11743
Phone: 631-424-0905, Fax: 631-424-4867
E-mail: info@gcmw.com
www.gcmw.com

GOLD COAST METAL WORKS
New York - Olomouc

Discriminating clients and design teams turn to Hedrick Brothers
Construction for exceptional craftsmanship and uncompromising service.
A tradition of excellence is built into new construction, renovation and
historic restoration projects throughout South Florida and Georgia.

HEDRICK
BROTHERS
CONSTRUCTION

HedrickBrothers.com | #WeAreBuilders

MAYFAIR
CONSTRUCTION

Architect: Oliver Cope
Photographer: Durston Saylor
Interior Designer: Eve Robinson Associates

SOME MIGHT ONLY SEE BRICKS.

BUT WE SEE SOMETHING DIFFERENT, GRANDER, NOBLER. WE SEE SOMETHING
THE ROMANS CREATED TO BUILD THEIR WORLD. AND WE SEE THE POTENTIAL
THEY LEFT US TO BUILD YOUR VISION.

GENERAL CONTRACTOR WORKING ANYWHERE YOU NEED US.
KREKOWJENNINGS.COM, 206 625 0505

FLOWER
CONSTRUCTION

FLOWCON.NET
(908) 219-4102

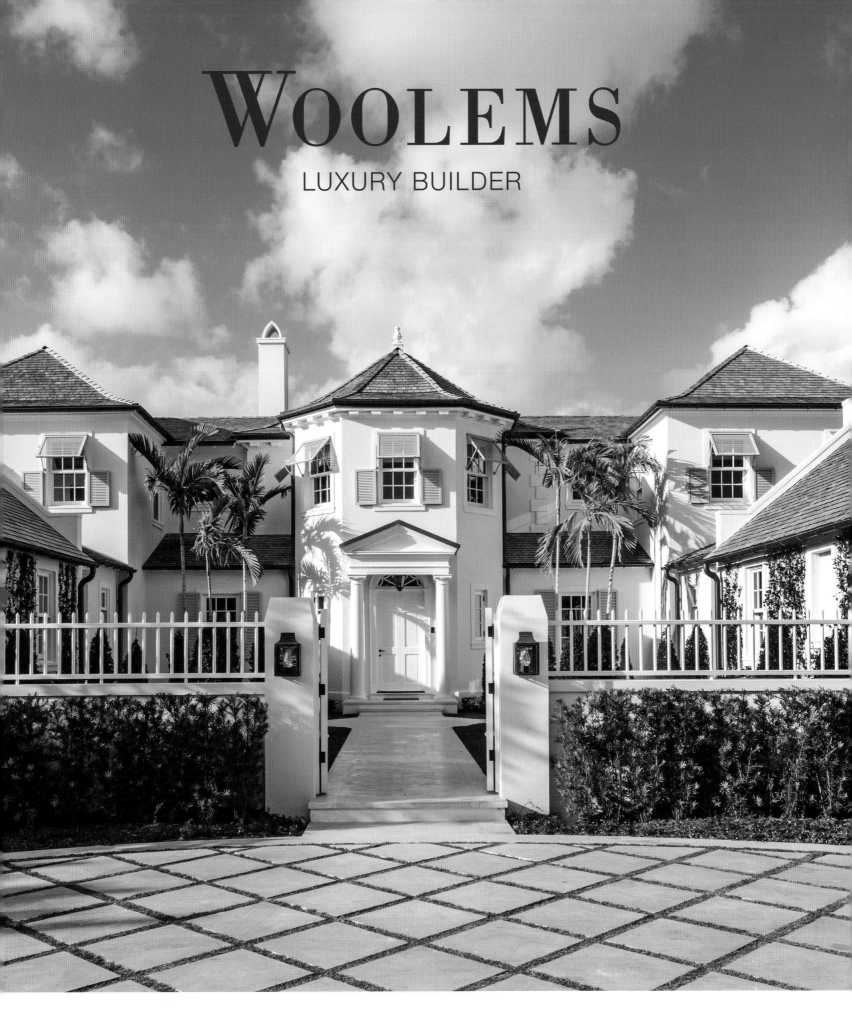

WOOLEMS

LUXURY BUILDER

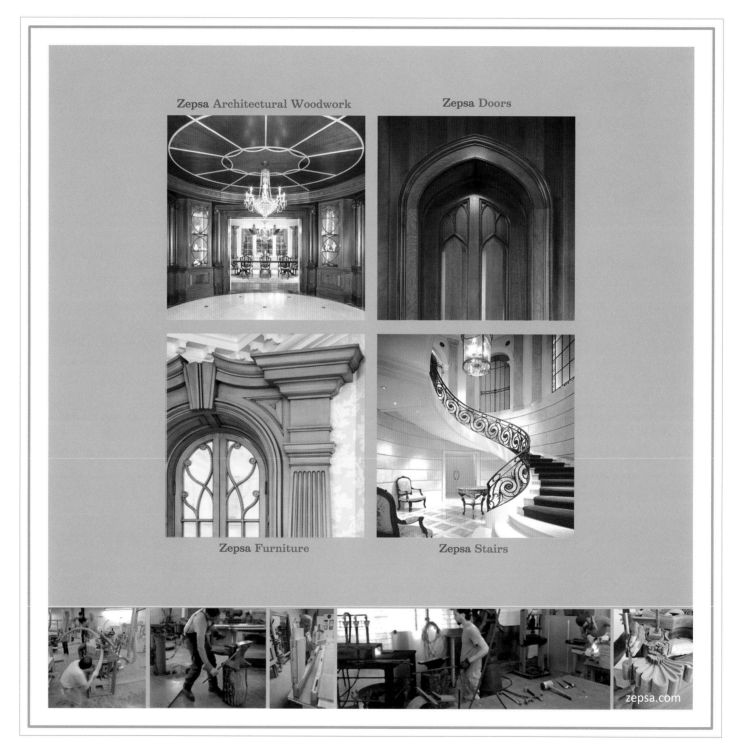

Zepsa Architectural Woodwork

Zepsa Doors

Zepsa Furniture

Zepsa Stairs

zepsa.com

Zepsa Industries

NEW YORK | CHARLOTTE | FLORIDA

Architectural Woodwork | Marine Interiors | Monumental Stairs | Custom Doors
Studio Furniture | Handmade Floors | Architectural Metalwork

SEBASTIAN
Construction Group

CRAFTSMANSHIP. PRIVACY. SECURITY.

ENHANCING & PROTECTING ARCHITECTURAL
MASTERPIECES NOW AND FOR GENERATIONS TO COME.

COMPASS
IRONWORKS

717-442-4500 | GAP, PA
WWW.COMPASSIRONWORKS.COM

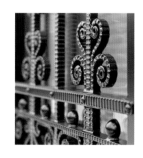

S.DONADIC INC

CONSTRUCTION MANAGEMENT

45-25 39TH STREET LONG ISLAND CITY NY 11104
WWW.DONADIC.COM

Griffith Observatory overlooking downtown Los Angeles. Photo: Anke Mackenthun